Westerlee
Delfland
Maasdijk
Gaag
MAASLAND
Ter Lucht
MAASSLUIS
Scheur
ROZENBURG
Calandkanaal
5e Petroleumhaven
Europoort
Hartelkanaal
7e Petroleumhaven
Oosterlandse Rak
Brielse Rak
BRIELLE
Rugge
Tinte
Brielse Meer
Brittanniëhaven
St. Laurenshaven
Seinehaven
Zwartewaal
Vierpolders

ILLUSTRA

RIJNMOND,
Rotterdam and the mouths of
the Rhine and Meuse

ISBN 90 6618 520 1

photographs and aerialphotographs:
Bart Hofmeester and
Dick Sellenraad
texts: Kees Stiksma
translation: Linda Korpel
editor: Dick van Koten
production: Peter de Raaf

colour separations:
Fokomon, Heerjansdam
type-setting: IGS, Rotterdam
printing and binding:
Brepols, Turnhout

*CIP-GEGEVENS KONINKLIJKE
BIBLIOTHEEK, DEN HAAG*

Hofmeester, Bart

*Rijnmond/Bart Hofmeester
(photogr.); Kees Stiksma (text);
(comp. by Dick van Koten);
transl. from the Dutch.
— Ridderkerk: Kopub. — Ill.,
photographs.
ISBN 90-6618-520-1 geb.
SISO zhol 986.6
UDC 914.926.17(084.12) UGI 760
Trefw.: Rijnmond; fotoboeken.*

Distribution, sales and promotion:
Multiboek BV, Rijsoord
(Ridderkerk)

Rijnmond

A photo-safari by

Bart Hofmeester & Dick Sellenraad

Text by

Kees Stiksma

Rotterdam and the mouths of the Rhine and Meuse

A book to read and a book to look leisurely through, depicting a restless area. The first book ever published about Rijnmond as a whole. Even without the text the book tells its story by means of photos about an area living from the water, cooperating with the water and recognizing its dependance on the water.

It is old land, with an ever changing aspect, however. When 'Rijnmond' is mentioned one often thinks of ports and ships, long freight-trains on a viaduct, a forest of tall chimneys and long lines of cars queueing in front of the Van Brienenoordbridge. People may even think that industry always has an unpleasant flavour...

Those who mention 'Rijnmond' do not immediately think of green polderland and cottages, sprawling behind huge protecting dykes, listening to the song of the sea... They will certainly not think of the vast dune area with its unique vegetation near Westvoorne.

Rijnmond is a synonym for big, busy, bustling, tall, high, noisy. It is true. Rijnmond – being the gateway to Europe – is economically the most important area of The Netherlands. The photos in this book speak clearly language.

But Rijnmond is more. Rijnmond may be silent and quiet, green, dreamy and lonely. There are towns and villages, where the walls and the cobbles tell us the history from times immemorial.

Page after page, this book tells us the story of people who transformed this moorland into a dwelling and working area, famous all over the world. The photographers visualized the traces people left in this area. The people themselves are present, indeed, but sometimes very small and very far away – tiny, compared with what they have created.

The performers change, the play goes on. Bart Hofmeester, Dick Sellenraad and Kees Stiksma watched with great respect what human hands created. They did it in a way which deserves our respect and attention.

André van der Louw
Chairman of Rijnmond

All rivers flow towards the sea. They always have and they continue to do so. So it is with the Rhine (Rijn) and the Meuse (Maas). They seem to have haphazardly chosen their way via a countless number of tributaries with just as many different names, through the delta of the Low Countries, out to the North Sea.
However, nature often charts a course which men disagree with. And so, as in the case of the people of Rotterdam, man lends nature a hand. More than a century ago, they constructed the New Waterway (Nieuwe Waterweg).

At the beginning of our present era, the Romans placed great value on the Rhine River as their military shipping route.
In the Middle Ages, this trade route came to signify a great deal to the up and coming third class, the merchants. And who could forget the hairraising stories of the blood-thristy, plundering Germanic pirates?
From the 15th to the 19th centuries the stretch between Amsterdam and Cologne (stock yards from the 16th century onwards) was heavily travelled. With the industrial developments in Germany's Ruhr area, Rotterdam, as transhipment port grew significantly after 1870.

The post World War II years saw the introduction of a new phase in industrial activity: barges.
Just as does the Rhine, the Meuse River takes its place in the international network of rivers. The Vienna Convention of 1815 allowed for the same freedom of navigation on the Meuse, as was already the case on the Rhine.

"Thinking of Holland, I see wide rivers sluggishly moving through unending lowland", said the poet Marsman in the opening words of "Memories of Holland". "Incessant floods have left their mark on the land of the great rivers."

Water: both friend and foe. In their incessant struggle, men and the water have made their marks on this unique section of The Netherlands. Though their names change from Rijn and Maas to Lek and Noord, as they meet at Kinderdijk, the rivers reach out to each other and merge to continue their journey together through the common bed of the New Meuse (Nieuwe Maas), Scheur and Nieuwe Waterweg out to the North Sea.

The Rijnmond! Rather curiously shown on maps as the mouth of the Maas. Here, ships from every sea in the world come to call. At every hour of the day and night they appear on the horizon. Box-shaped boats containing new cars, highly stacked container ships, quick-moving coasters, low-lying tankers, bulk carriers bearing ore, grain and coal – the riches of the earth. Maasvlakte, Europoort, Botlek: import, transit and export, trade and industry. Here, and along the lower course of the big rivers fiercely beats the economic heart of The Netherlands.

Rijnmond, the golden clasp on the silver belt of The Netherlands is more than just a seaport of world renown. Sometimes breathtaking, in the literal sense of the word but always so in the figurative sense.
No matter how the winds of trade may blow, Rijnmond resolutely heads toward a better future.

We now request the pleasure of your company on our photo-safari, as we make our way through Rijnmond. You will surely be convinced that Rijnmond is more than just the world port of Rotterdam.
Bon voyage!

ROTTERDAM SOUTH SHORE

Noordzee

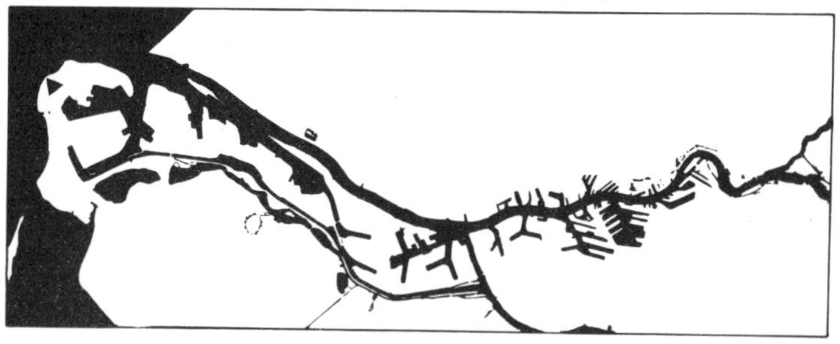

The arms of the northern and southern block-dams are open night and day to ships from all over the world, offering a welcome and facilitating a speedy return.

This photo-safari begins on a beautiful evening at the mouth of the Maas River near Hoek van Holland. The North Sea shows her most friendly face. The sun hides behind a small cloud, giving the evening a red hue. A gentle breeze ripples the surface of the sea, as if she is pleased with our proposed expedition. There are no breakers to speak of.
Soft waves stream up over the beach, romping playfully with the concrete blocks of the Northern and Southern Dams (Noorder- en Zuiderdam). It appears as if the blocks were carelessly flung down by some giant in a playful mood. In fact, these two dams are an engineering masterpiece.
The North Sea does not always put her best foot forward. During autumn or when unpredicted storms arise, this same sea can recklessly lash the coast. This is when she shows her rage, to the point of causing the coastal population to hold its breath.
1 February 1953, the date of the flood disaster, which cost so many lives and caused immeasurable material damage, is far from being forgotten.
Now both dams act as open arms in which Rotterdam holds onto navigation as a spoiled child.

The 850 meter wide channel between the two dams allows ample passage of 4 large sea-going vessels at once, without involving any complicated manoeuvres. The draught of the largest ship, plus the excess depth necessary for safe navigation, determines the depth of the channel.
Sand, in large amounts, is continually carried into the mouth of the Maas River with the tide, thereby threatening the draught. Therefore, it is no wonder that dredging must constantly take place, not in the least to the dismay of the dredgers.
Between the Noorder- and the Zuiderdams there originated a spacious outer harbour with entrance ways to the New Waterway (Nieuwe Waterweg) and to the Maasvlakte and Europoort. The entrance ways are separated from each other by a division dam. This is superb for mammoth tankers, who need lengthy routes for breaking distances, for which a calm channel is necessary.
A further consideration is the regulation of waterborne traffic. The Rotterdam Port Authority is housed in the Europoint complex on Marconiplein in Rotterdam-West. The Port Coordination Centre is also located in this ''nerve centre'' of the harbour. The Master Control Room is where the operational services are coordinated.

Continuous dredging is necessary to maintain the required depth of the fairway.
The captain's room of the harbour company of the Rotterdam municipality is the nerve centre of the harbour. It is from this point that the incoming ships are shown their berths.

8 Maasmond

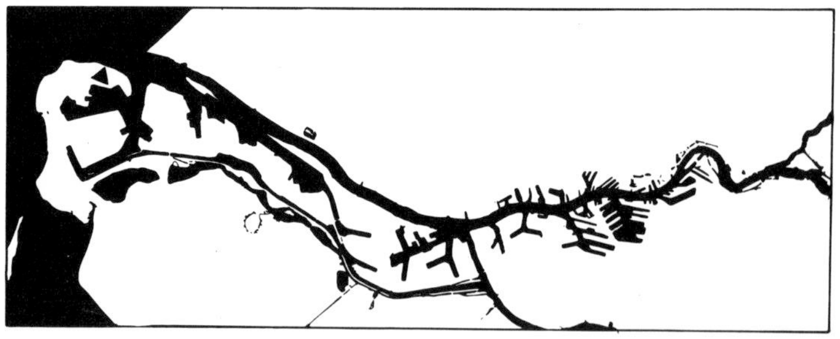

The helicopter over the tanks indicates that piloting is carried out by the most modern methods. The chain of radar stations of 1956 have recently been replaced.
A broken supertanker needs careful manoeuvering and an exceptional number of tugs.

An indispensable link in traffic safety are the Government Pilotage Services, which are assigned the duties of piloting into the mouth of the harbour, on the lower course of the major rivers and on the canals, which have been made accessible for shipping. In addition they are responsible for the maintenance of seaway crossroads, using pilots boats and for the piloting station in the harbour.
The most modern methods are used for piloting ships into the port. Helicopters are often used to lower pilots onto the ships even before they reach the mouth of the harbour. When fog or other adverse weather conditions exist, waterborne traffic on the rivers is assisted in every way possible. To further this aim a chain of radar stations was built along the Nieuwe Waterweg in 1956. Currently a new shorebased radar system is under construction, consisting of one Central Post, three regional stations and a chain of new radar posts. This will be joined to the traffic stations by micro-wave links. This Vessel Traffic Management System covers from the Nieuwe Maas up to the Van Brienenoord brug.
One part of the division dam in the harbour mouth is the Scheur haven. This is the home port for Europoort's harbour tug boats. In fact they are sometimes used for quite unusual jobs.

Maasvlakte

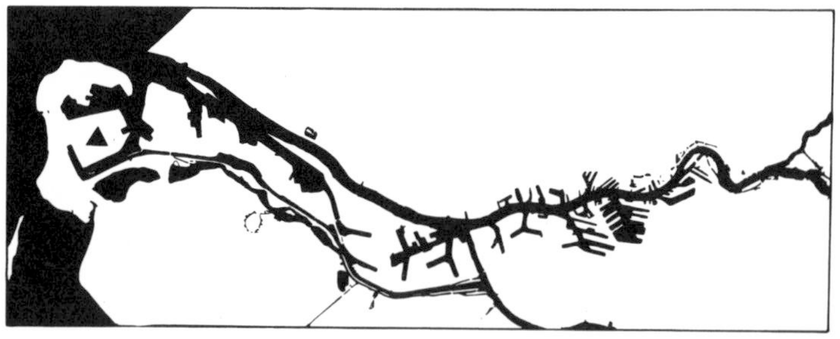

Their geographical position, on the mouths of three rivers – Rhine (Rijn), Meuse (Maas) and Scheldt (Schelde) – makes the Dutch what they are by nature: traders and sailors.
Formerly the only natural resource was the earth itself, which was intensively cultivated for agricultural purposes.

The "Gateway to Europe" could now call itself the world's largest port. The great westward expansion had begun: from Pernis to Botlek, then from Botlek to Europoort and finally from Europoort to the Maasvlakte.
The Maasvlakte, wrested from the sea, came about by land reclamation projects and damming off the surrounding coastal shoals. Since 1966 it is a harbour and industrial area which several large companies, including Maasvlakte Oil Terminal, Europees Massagoed Overslagbedrijf (EMO) and British Petroleum Raffinaderij Nederland call "home".

The Netherlands fast became a junction of busy trade routes. They don't call the Dutch ''the freight carriers of Europe'' for nothing, you know!
In the days following Napoleon's empire, Rotterdam gradually grew to be the most important seaport in Western Europe.
The Mannheim Treaty of 1868 guaranteed free passage for all ships on the Rhine.
The onset of the Industrial Age saw a rapid expansion of the Rotterdam harbours and by 1872, when the construction of the New Waterway (Nieuwe Waterweg) was completed, there was no way of stopping the continuous progress.

This has not changed, although there are now available more natural resources than was ever formerly imagined.
However, in the Maas plain (Maasvlakte) and in the New Waterway (Nieuwe Waterweg) area this image deserves some re-appraisal, as here in the principal world port beats the heart of The Netherlands as an industrial nation.

12

Maasvlakte

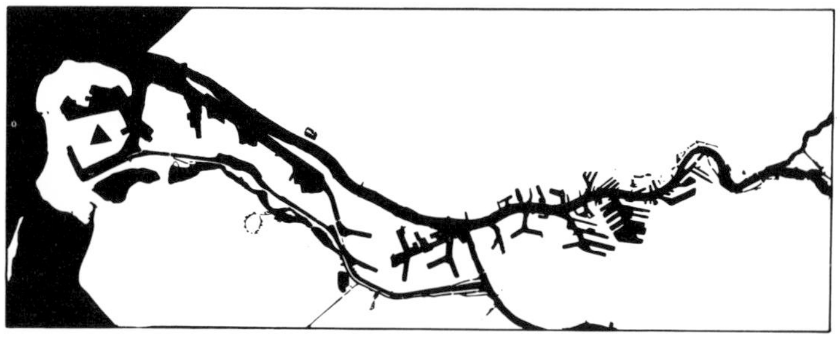

ECT – Europe Container Terminus; household words in the world of modern shipping.
The Deltaterminal on the Maas plain, with its railway connections and 1200 m quay on a plot of 810,000 m², is the most complete terminal.

Here are the first 2 of ECT's container gantry cranes in action. Each crane has a 46 meter span. Six of these colossal pieces of equipment are scheduled to be built. In fact it could be up to seven by now because building projects like these change, often multiplying from day to day. With the 1,200 meter long quayside there is certainly room for more. The 800,000 sq.m. site looks rather empty and abandoned on this picture, but between the time the photograph was taken and the publishing of this book, it will undoubtedly be fuller and the rows of containers soon be highly stacked, covering the site.

By all means, do not underestimate the size of one of these containerships and, as a means of comparison, notice the ship next to it and the one in the lower right hand corner, just barely in the picture.

The EMO in action! A narrow dam separates the Missisippihaven from the Hartelhaven, with its oreloading installation for pushboat units. Rail transport of iron-ore to the hinterland is also widely used. A transport tunnel enables coal to be transported from EMO directly to the Municipal Electricity Company's power station. A contract has been drawn up between the Municipality of Rotterdam and Koninklijke Maatschappij ''De Schelde'' for radical renovation. The power station has, up until now been fed by oil or gas, but dependent on weather conditions, coal will be used as much as possible in the near future. A sum of Dfl. 400 million has already been spent for the boilers alone. Should you loose your way on the expanse of the Maasvlakte, just use the high chimneys to get your bearing. The 8th Petroleumhaven supplies the power station with cooling water which, after use is then carried away through a cooling pond into the lagoon between the concrete-block dam and the beach.

In the Missisippi Harbour the greatest ore ships are unloaded by the EMO (Europese Massagoedoverslagbedrijf), the European mass merchandise transhipment. And of course coal. The reconstruction of a transport tunnel will enable the coal to be transported directly to the power station.

Europoort

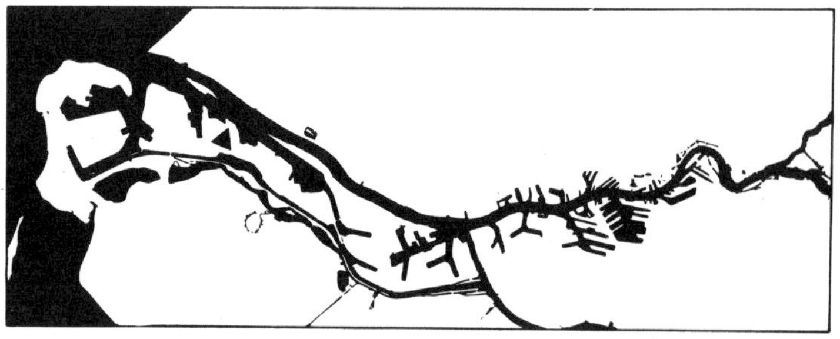

The Calandkanaal is separated from the Nieuwe Waterweg by an elongated peninsula. This canal links the 4th, 5th and 7th Petroleum Harbours in Europoort with the North Sea and the Hinterland.

The distance from Maasvlakte to Europoort is quickly covered by car. An excellent highway system connects both harbour complexes with one another and with Rotterdam and the hinterland. The Beneluxhaven, 4th, 5th and 7th Petroleumhaven are linked to the North Sea and the hinterland by the Calandkanaal.

Located at the Beneluxhaven are, among others, the terminals for North Sea Ferries' ro-ro ships, the rapid, daily connection between Rotterdam and Hull (England). The GEM (Graan Elevator Maatschappij) is a modern grain storage and transhipment company, handling sea-going vessels weighing up to 200,000 tons. The hydraulic vacuum cranes have an enormous discharging capacity. Smaller ships and coasters bound for further inland European ports are loaded on the sea side; for Rhine barges there are loading facilities in the adjacent Dintelhaven.

The 7th Petroleumhaven is the harbour situated the farthest to the east and handles VLCCs and ULCCs (very-large and ultra-large crude carriers). The Koeweit Raffinaderij (originally property of Gulf) is located here, as well. The new owners have recently decided to invest Dfl. 200 million in this refinery.

Here in the Benelux Harbour, next to the Kuwait Petroleum Company (Gulf in former days), we find the Grain Elevator Company (GEM, Graan Elevator Maatschappij), an ultra-modern shipping company for grain and derivatives. Ocean-going vessels of up to 200,000 tons dw are being loaded and unloaded here.

Europoort

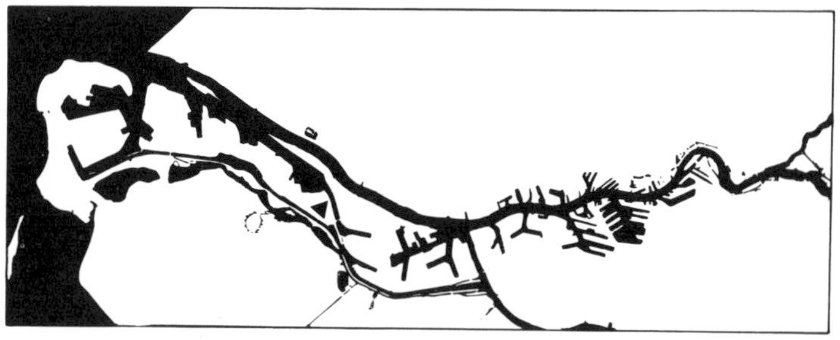

At the end of the Calandkanaal we see the Calandbrug, its four concrete lifting towers a landmark in the vastness of Europoort. Its wind resistance causes considerable problems and, in order to facilitate a safe passage through the bend to the bridge, a gigantic wind break is being built.

We leave the Europoort by way of the bridge called Calandbrug. With its four concrete lifting towers it has surely become an eye-catcher in this vast area of land and water. The bridge separates Europoort from Botlek. The movable portion weighing 2,600 tons, is raised 38 meters within one minute and achieves a safe passage of 50 meters.
Here, oil is the order of the day. Various tank parks are grouped around the 7th Petroleumhaven. The tanks store oil products for further transport, either by pipeline to the hinterland or by tanker to more distant European destinations.

The building of tankparks is very specialized work. For the foundation of each tank, a tank mound must first be put up. The tank is then built on top. Often the storage capacity measures 100,000 cubic meters.
It's no wonder, then, that these parks with their highly flammable contents are subject to such strict safety requirements. Those who build these gigantic installations look like ants in comparison.
A complicated network of computer-controlled pipelines regulates the transport to and from the tanks.

Building a tank installation is a specialized job. A mound is created for the tank foundation and, for safety, the tanks are surrounded by bunds. The pipeline is controlled by an advanced computerised system.

Rozenburg

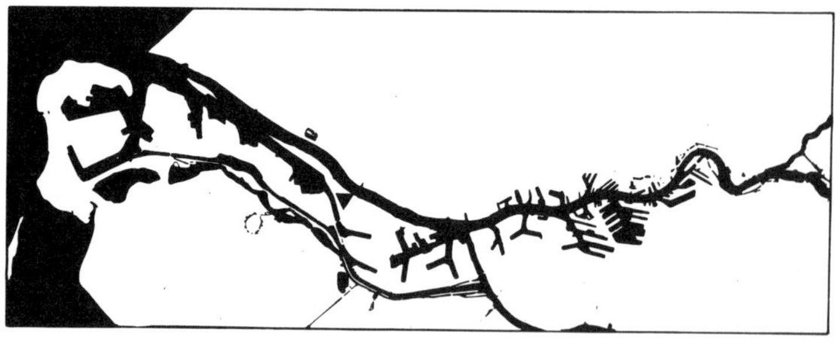

Geographically constrained within two sources of national prosperity – Botlek and Europoort – is Rozenburg, which with only a small area available for housing is almost overwhelmed by the surrounding oil tanks.

Pushed away to the outermost northwestern corner of Botlek, lies Rozenburg, like a green oasis hemmed in by artificially raised industrial areas and dikes.
Until 1 January 1980, practically all of the Europoort area belonged to this municipality. Then, Rotterdam annexed it.
Geographically constrained between two sources of national prosperity – Botlek and Europoort – Rozenburg is forced to make due with the land on which its residential area is built and a strip of land between the Nieuwe Maas, Waterweg, Scheur and Calandkanaal. Talk about feeling suffocated: just imagine being surrounded by oil tanks!
The Rozenburgse Boulevard is the main dam of the village, which was originally situated at polder-level. It has been disguised as a park complete with children's playgrounds.

Next to the Esso refineries the thirsty oil-seekers are drilling to find new oil sources. Cheaper exploration could hardly be possible, nor could the supply line be shorter. For these Dutch, oil is not next door, but under the floor!

The thirst for oil is unquenchable everywhere in the world, even here. Just as refineries sprung out of the ground like toadstools in the post-war years, oil is miraculously springing out of the ground here. Right next to the Esso refinery thirsty experts drill for new sources of oil. The Dutch couldn't ask for a closer supply than their own backyard!

Botlek

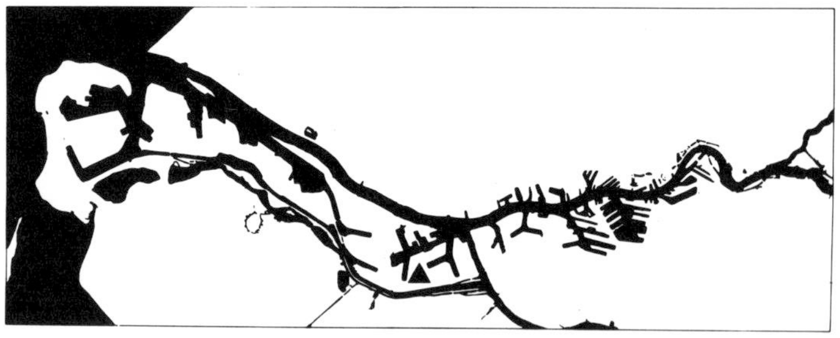

The impressive Botlek basin with the third Petroleum port, the Chemicals port and the St. Laurent port as the most important gateways.
Here we find amongst others, the refineries and petrochemical plants of Esso.
Here also are Dow, Paktank and Aluchemie.

There, where the name of the New Meuse River (Nieuwe Maas) changes to Het Scheur, lies Botlek: an ambitious and bustling port area. The following harbours: Geul, 3rd Petroleum, Welplaat, Chemie, St. Laurens, Toronto, 2nd and 1st Werkhaven make up this impressive complex. The 3rd Petroleum harbour deals with oil, oil and more oil. Esso Nederland, with its huge refinery and petrochemical plant looms above its fellow occupants on this harbour, although Dow Chemical, Paktank and Nieuw Matex are also clearly visible. The harbour can accomodate tankers up to 60,000 dWt (dead weight tonnage). Along the Chemiehaven, Panocean Tank Storage has extensive tank parks. Akzo Chemie has quite a complex here as well. Verolme Cleaning and Verolme Botlek, on the 2nd and 1st Werkhaven are our last stop on the tour of Botlek. A bit obscured by the haze, lies Vlaardingen, on the opposite side of Het Scheur. The second-largest city in the Rijnmond region, Vlaardingen is a port and industrial city with a new, lively downtown area. In times gone by, it was an important fishing village, though fishing has all but faded out of the picture now.

The enormous shipping company of Frans Swarttouw draws attention from afar.
Two 90,000 t ships can be unloaded simultaneously.
A conveyor system runs directly to the barges.

G.E.M. (Graan Elevator Maatschappij), the Grain Elevator Company is located at the head of the Botlek turret. The silo complex and pier, with its permanent elevators attract one's attention from far away.
At this pier, two 90,000 ton bulk-carriers can be unloaded simultaneously. A synchronized conveyor-belt system allows for continuous loading of Rhine barges alongside the pier or for storage in the silos. Floating elevators often lend a helping hand. At the corner of Botlek - St. Laurenshaven, Frans Swarttouw and his neighbour E.M.O. - Botlek (Europees Massagoed Overslagbedrijf) have their facilities.

Botlek

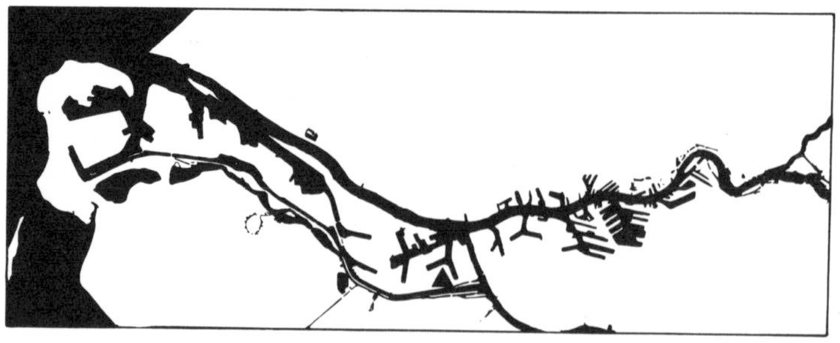

At the site of the Esso refinery a flexicoker is being built. It will be powered by the heaviest oil particles, the residue from vacuum distillation. This is the third of this type of installation in the world, and the first for the Exxon company.

Esso Nederland has a refinery at the 3rd Petroleumhaven. Here, they are investing huge sums of money in the building of a so-called flexicoker.
The total investment involves over Dfl. 2½ billion.
The actual work on the project began in 1983 and is scheduled for completion in 1986. The construction phase of the project currently provides employment for 1,200 and will, at its peak time employ a work force of 4,000.
The Flexicoker is "fed" with the blackest of oil particles – the residue from vacuum distillation. This installation is the third of its kind in the world: the first but undoubtedly not the last, for the world-wide Exxon concern. It goes without saying how much this project means to the Dutch economy.
The Hartelkanaal connects the harbour industries of Maasvlakte, Europoort and Botlek with the hinterland: an important shipping connection for Rhine and other inland navigation.
This canal has open access to the Old Meuse River (Oude Maas). Powerful push tugs thrust four to six barges, each containing 3,000 tons of freight, to the Ruhr area.

Powerful vessels can propel four or six barges laden with at least 3,000 t. of ore along the Hartelkanaal to the Ruhr. This busy Rhine and inland waterway runs along the Oude Maas, and not through Rotterdam.

Pernis

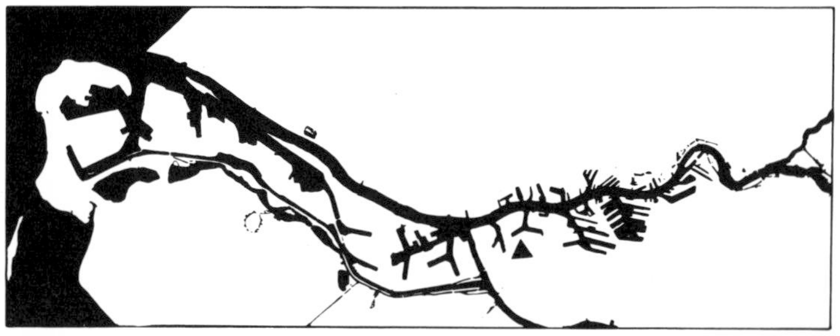

The two tall central chimneys (213 m) on the site of the 1st and 2nd Petroleum port, dominated by Shell, but also represented by Texaco, are very striking. There has been considerable reduction in air pollution since many of the lower chimneys have become redundant.

Adieu Botlek, bonjour Pernis! With our camera bags full of impressions of "the indescribable magnitude of Rijnmond", we dive under the Oude Maas via the Botlektunnel: at least 25 meters under sea level, by the way. This tunnel measures 500 meters from shore to shore.
The petrochemical industries, situated near the 1st and 2nd Petroleumhaven are dominated by Shell, although Texaco makes its presence visible in no small way. Shell's two soaring central chimney stacks (213 meter high) are prominent landmarks. They replace a large number of lower chimneys which used to emit harmful industrial gasses. These industrial gasses bounced against a 100 meter high reverse air flow with all of its unpleasant consequences. The amount of air polution is considerably less since these higher chimneys are being used.
An evening look at Shell offers a fascinating view.
The flare marks the radiating centre point of a spectacular scene.

Hoogvliet is another part of the Rotterdam agglomeration. Bordered on the West by the Oude Maas and on the East by Poortugaal and heavily reliant on the harbour for employment, this residential city will, in the future, become a part of the new community of Albrandswaard.

At night the Shell installation near Pernis is so spectacular a sight as to detract from the possibility of nasal irritation.

Eemhaven

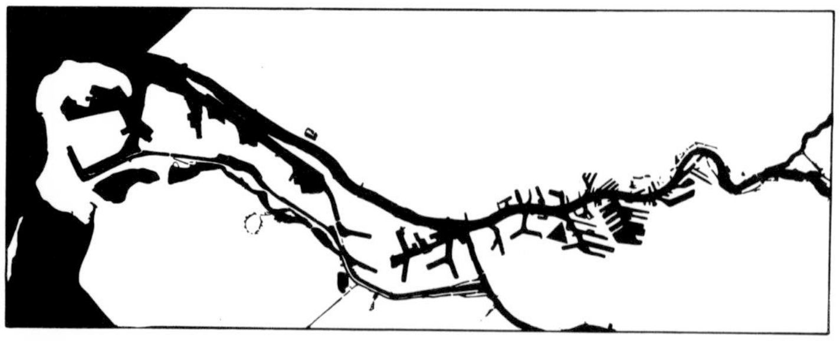

The Prinses Margriet port and the Prins Willem Alexander port are part of the Eem harbour area. It is here that the Europe Container Terminus (ECT) has its home terminus. Nowadays world shipping is unthinkable without containerisation.

The Eemhaven-complex, east of Pernis, by way of its various ports: Prinses Margriet haven, Prins Willem Alexander haven, Prinses Beatrix haven and Prins Johan Friso haven links two generations of the Dutch royal family. These bustling ports predominately handle containers. ECT, Europe Container Terminus bv, for example has its home terminal here. ECT, founded in 1967, handles about a million containers a year.
At the home terminal, this ever-expanding container transshipment company grew from small-scale to its current proportions.

The international transportation world can no longer function without containers. Giant container ships line the quays, where ingenious loading and unloading facilities and sky-high stacks of containers, waiting to be transported, together conjure up a merry assortment of colors on a glittering pallet.
Stevedoring Company Quick Dispatch, Seaport Terminals and the Municipal Electricity Company's main power plant at Waalhaven (GEB) form a picturesque background against which these activities take place.

Attention is caught by the gigantic container ships along the quays, ingenious lightering facilities on the quayside, and containers piled sky-high. A reduction of two hours from the former sailing time has made the Maas delta more competitive.

Waalhaven

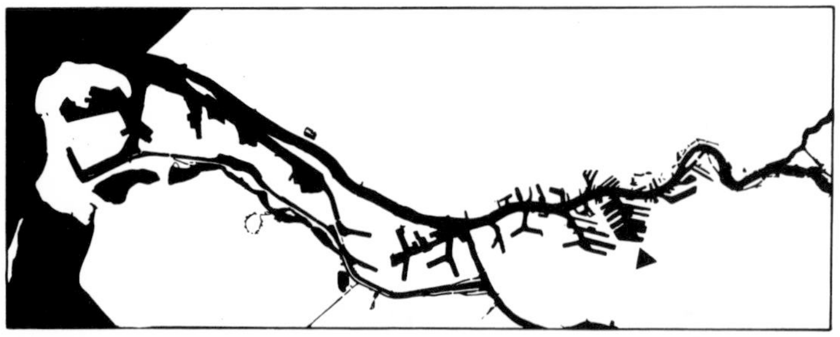

The preceding pages might give the impression that chemicals, containers, grain, coal and oil constitute the whole range of activities of the Maas delta, Europoort and Botlek. The Waalhaven basin shows that this is not so.

Should the previous pages have given the impression that chemicals, containers, grain and fodder, coal and oil on Maasvlakte, in Europoort, Botlek and the Pernis-area make up the largest part of the activity in the Greater Rotterdam Port Area, nothing is farther from the truth. Closer to home, the Waalhaven buzzes with activity. This harbour basin, a first-rate general cargo port, is a busy beehive day and night. Pier 1 handles the supply and distribution of wood and wood products. Pier 2 is a good example of a multi-purpose terminal with a surprising variety in types of cargo. Beyond Pier 3 the Waalhaven offers berths for LASH-ships (lighter aboard the ship), while FLASH-and SPLASH boats also call at this port. There is, in addition a docking area for large ro-ro ships.

We could continue, endlessly, to name all the activities which take place in the Waalhaven but let's leave it at these few examples and continue southward. Now occupied by industries with no quayside facilities, this area was the site of the Waalhaven airport prior to World War II.
The Waalhaven offers a spectacular evening panorama. Against a nighttime-blue sky, the high towering cranes look more like finely spun lace.

In the Waalhaven basin we find a general cargo port of the highest standard.
At night the lights of the tower cranes suggest a fairly-land; during the day the most heterogeneous vessels sail along the Maas in front of the Waalhaven.

30

Maashaven

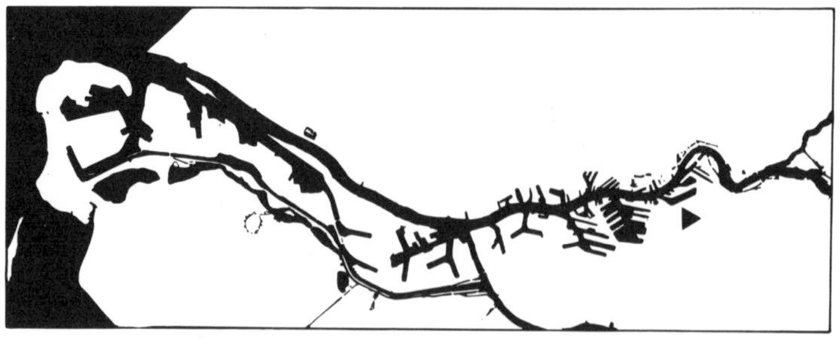

Here are the most important components of this busy port; the ocean-going ships in their berths and the towering cranes on the quayside, the barges and their masters awaiting their cargo.

This is a view of the Maashaven, but is a very typical scene for all of the harbours in Rotterdam-South which came into existence in the years between World War I and World War II. Though overshadowed by the vastness of Maasvlakte, Europoort and Botlek this harbour area still projects an energetic and even more varied picture.

Moored ocean-going vessels and cranes stretching skyward are still to be found by the quayside. Rhine barge masters awaiting their loads and general cargo still dominate the scene. Small is beautiful is the theme song here. Don't be mistaken – bulk goods and pushing barges are also around, but clearly the accent is on a smaller-scale.

As the 20th century approached, a period of great property for trade and industry was dawning. At this point, Rotterdam experienced a heretofore unsurpassed population explosion. Whereas the population numbered 100,000 in the year 1850, by 1900 that figure was up to 300,000 and in 1915 it had risen to over 450,000. This growth originated, for the most part in the rural areas, especially the islands of South Holland and of Zeeland, and the province of Brabant.
This helped to make Rotterdam what it is today and established the city's reputation as a world port.

Step by step old Rotterdam has been transformed. The longshoreman seen here is a true descendant of the founders of modern Rotterdam, who could be justifiably proud of their achievements.

32

Nieuwe Maas, Rijnhaven

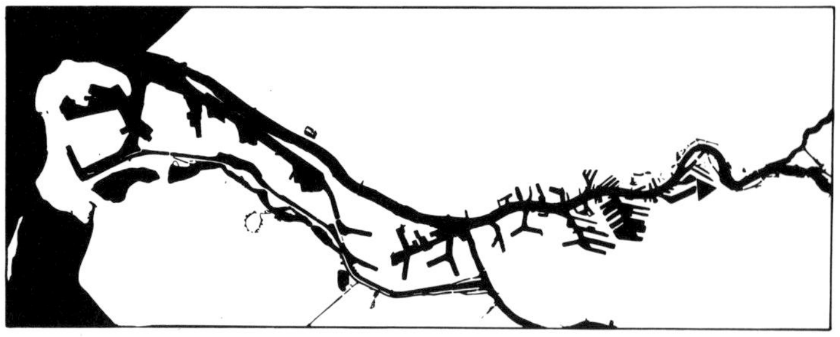

Heavily-laden with bulk cargo, moored barges line the shore of Noordereiland.
To the left, behind the Port Authority Building lie the Innerport (Binnenhaven) and the Railwayport (Spoorweghaven). They have had their day and are now being transformed into modern housing areas.
On Katendrecht, port facilities recall the glorious days of the Holland America Lines (HAL's luxurious passenger ships).
The Euromast is the landmark on the right bank of the Maas, towering over the stark, white medical university building.

From the lifting towers of the railway bridge over the Koningshaven the view to both east and west is fascinating. Behind the Poortgebouw (to the left) are the inner port and the Railway port. Their day is past, and they are now being transformed into housing areas.

Spoorweghaven, Binnenhaven

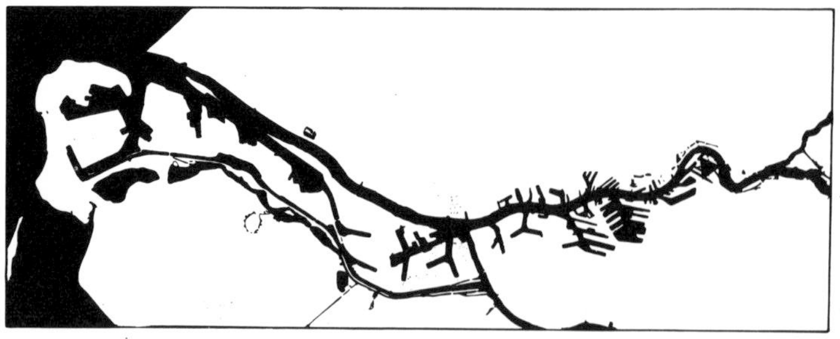

From these same lifting towers we see the railway, the last image of the southern shore, running south to Brabant. The steam-tram running to the Isles used to start from this point. This line brought a whole army of people seeking employment in the second half of the 19th century.

Whatever one may think of the 19th century Mr. L. Pincoffs (who later turned out to be a forger and fled to America), his impetuous nature contributed a great deal to the development of Rotterdam-South in the years 1870-1880. The most important step was the building of bridges, in 1874, connecting Rotterdam-South with the right bank of the Meuse River.
In the years that followed, steam trams left the Rosestraat huffing and puffing their way round winding bends towards the quiet villages and little-known neighbourhoods of the South Holland islands, even as far as Schouwen-Duiveland. The city now has other things in mind for this former tram route.
New housing areas arose where old harbour facilities and the shunting-yard of the Netherlands Railroad had closed down. Kijfhoek, near Zwijndrecht is the present shunting-yard.
The apartment complex on Rosestraat, nicknamed ''Paperclip'' because of the shape of its buildings, is a well-known, modern landmark. To the right of this area, are the Entrepothaven, the Binnenhaven and the Spoorweghaven. These harbours have lost much of their influence and will probably eventually disappear.

NORTH SHORE

Rotterdam-centrum, Blaak

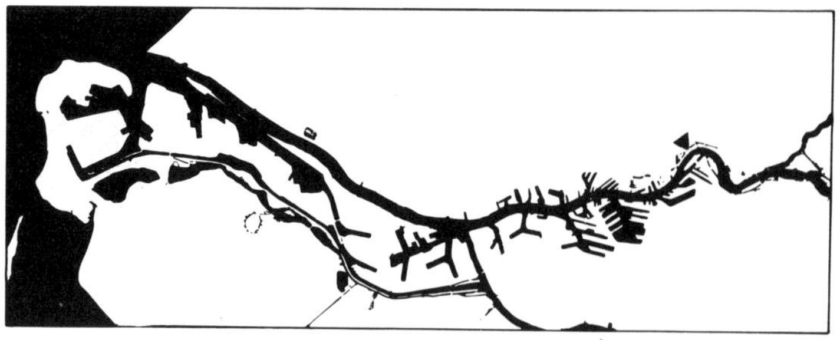

The North-South stretches of railroad and highway appear to have been constructed with a straight edge.
In fact, the railwaybridge is nearly ready for retirement, following over 100 years of faithful service. A few years from now, it will be replaced by a tunnel.
The Willemsbrug with its 5-lanes for traffic, 2 wide bicycle paths and spacious sidewalks is a sight to behold. As tightly strung as violin strings, the cables give the bridge a very contoured look. From this vantage point, the horizontal style of building makes Rotterdam appear stalwart and spacious.

The railway bridge has nearly finished its duty, after over a hundred years of service. The building of the railway tunnel will leave the Willembrug to its own reflections.

Rotterdam-centrum, Leuvehaven

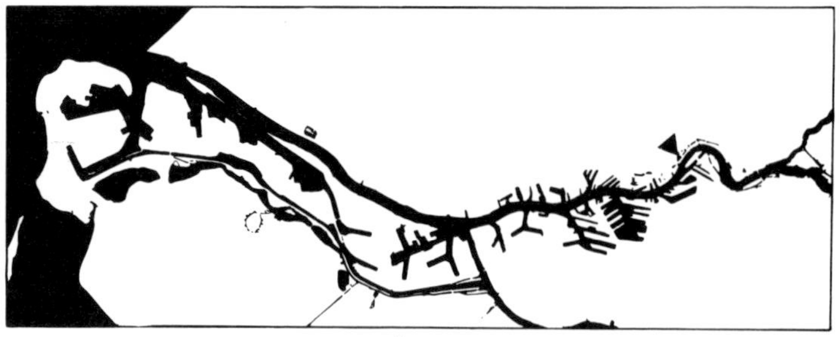

Yet, Rotterdam, hub of international traffic, is much more than a nerve centre for shipping, trade and industry.
The hustle and bustle in Rotterdam is not only in its harbours.
The city itself is alive with culture and entertainment, as well.

Over the Noordereiland and the Nieuwe Maas the metropolis shows itself as one entity. The ''Gateway to Europe'' is linked to the Earth's farthest corners by innumerable, invisible threads.

Parkhaven

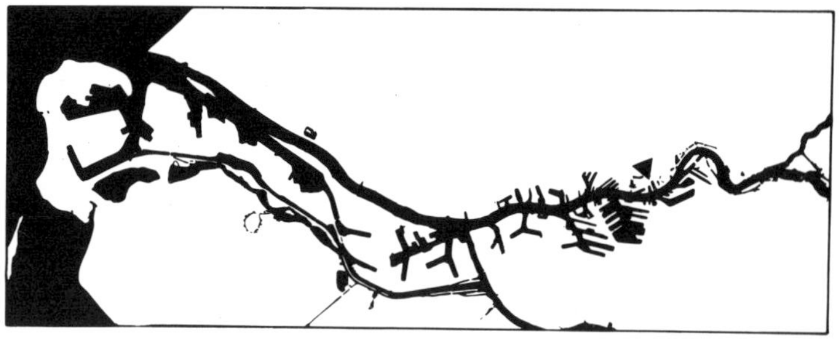

For the inland shipping, the Parksluices form the connection between the Nieuwe Maas and the Coolhaven. Formerly Parkhaven was here with the Batavierlijn which offered a regular service with London. There was no Euromast then.

The Parkhaven had lost some of its significance compared to the days, long ago, when it served as the point of departure for the Batavier Lines, a regular route between Rotterdam and London. On a clear day the 200 m high Euromast affords a panoramic view of the harbours and the North Sea. The building with the curved roof is the Government Tax Office, located on the Puntegaalstraat.

Continuing our photo-safari through Rijnmond on the right bank of the Maas in Rotterdam, we take the Maastunnel in the northerly direction. The building with the green, round roof belongs to the Maastunnel. This was the first underwater tunnel in The Netherlands. Construction began on 15 June 1937. When war broke out in The Netherlands on 10 May 1940 there were 5 concrete elements alongside the pier in the Waalhaven. The tunnel was first used on 14 February 1942 but there was no cause for celebration in Rotterdam. On 19 May 1945 the Maastunnel was officially opened. Huge grain silos loom in the background, remembrances of years gone by, when the storage of grain played and important role in the harbour.

Whether tinged a silver-grey by hazy light, or tinted blue by the sun shining through the scurrying clouds, the Maas, with its ever-changing scene, is always fascinating.
Beyond the hurrying barges, the Maashaven dreams of its glorious past.

Merwehaven, Lekhaven, IJselhaven

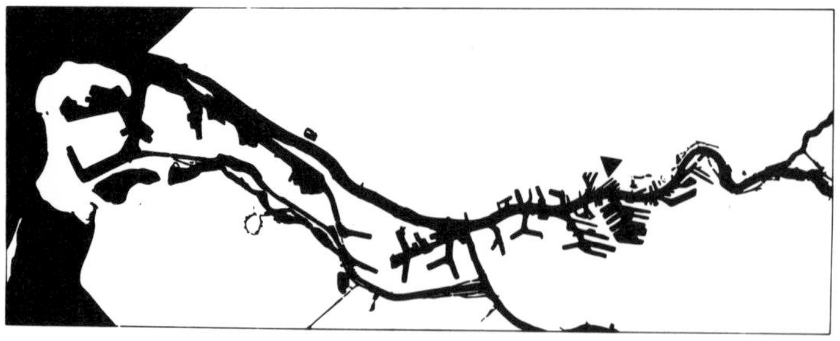

The towing service appeals to almost everybody. In the Netherlands towing came into being in the first half of the nineteenth century. It was then that steam-tugs offered assistance to sailors, leading them safely into the estuary.

In 1842 a certain Mr. Fop Smit, shipbuilder and owner of a shipping company in Kinderdijk, was granted a concession for a towing service in the South Holland and Zeeland seas. After his death, in 1866, his sons took over, founding L. Smit & Co. This harbour towing service led to the development in 1892 of the ocean towing service. Smit's company transported much of the Nederlands' dredging material to all corners of the world.
The competitor, Internationale Sleepdienst and the Smits merged and in 1923, Smit & Co's Internationale Sleepdienst was the result. Their working together with Van der Tak's Berging led to Smit taking them over, too. To make a long story short, Smit Internationale N.V. of Rotterdam is one of the largest Dutch towing companies, which has helped to make Dutch ocean tugs famous the world over.
The harbour businesses, such as ''Smit Zweden'' account for roughly 30% of the concern's profits. Now that's something to brag about!

Between Delfshaven and Schiedam are: Keilehaven (to the far left), IJsselhaven (above), and Lekhaven (below). These are typical examples of general cargo ports, as is shown by the unloading of apples at the fruit terminal.

Near the centre of Rijnmond, in the area of Marconiplein, where the striking Eurpoint-complex which draws so much attention and where the Municipal Port Management for the city of Rotterdam is housed, lie Keilehaven, Lekhaven and IJsselhaven. The Koushaven belongs to this complex as well. This harbour basin, jammed in between Delfshaven and Schiedam is a typical harbour which handles general cargo. Along the quays of the Lekhaven the names of Brazil, Uruguay, Levant, Argentina, and Pakistan take our thoughts to far away lands with which The Netherlands has trading ties. From these harbours, all sorts of staple products find their way inland to other Western European destinations. Rotterdam can rightly claim the title of Europe's Distribution Centre.

Schiedam, Wiltonhaven

The situation in ship-building and ship repair is critical. The shipyard, Wilton-Fijenoord, and the port of the same name, deal with this crisis. But what is the use of a world harbour without repair facilities?

Rapid expansion of the already existent industries such as shipbuilding and other metal industries took place along the lower course of the big rivers, following World War II.
At the present time, shipbuilding and ship repair yards in Rijnmond are facing a very serious crisis. In fact, 1976 was the last good year, except for a slight recovery in 1981. Since then things have sharply declined. The Wilton-Feijenoord shipyard in Schiedam, located on the harbour bearing the same name, almost painfully recalls the glorious years of Dutch shipbuilding. However, without adequate repair facilities, an important international port is like a one-armed man. Where will things go from here? Only the future can tell.

Vlaardingen, Maassluis

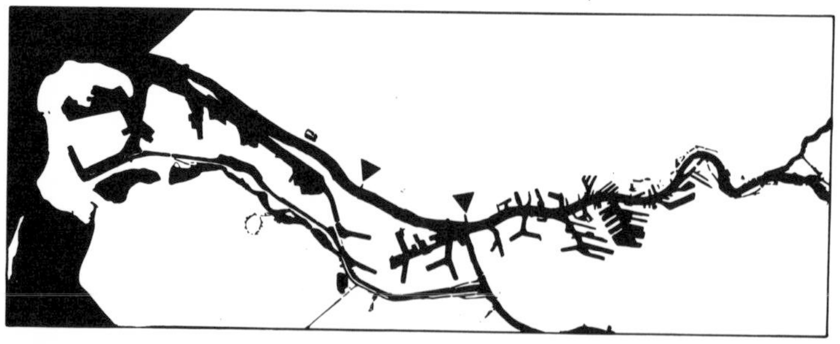

Two smaller harbours can be seen on the northern shore of the Nieuwe Waterweg: Vlaardingen (at top and in the upper right-hand corner) and Maassluis (in the lower right-hand corner). The most important harbour is the Vulcaanhaven.

Meanwhile our photo-safari has lead us along the Nieuwe Maas to the dry shores of Vlaardingen. The Vulcaanhaven is occupied by 2 companies: Havenbedrijf Vlaardingen-Oost (H.V.O.) and Frans Swarttouw Havenbedrijf.

In his time, they say Frans Swarttouw was a man who was not afraid of getting his hands dirty, referring to the type of work his company does.

The Outer Harbour (Buitenhaven) between East and West Harbours (Oost- and Westhavenkade) has open access to the ocean channel. Once the Nieuwe Waterweg was opened up, Vlaardingen's importance as a port dwindled. This city is the educational and cultural heart of the region.

In the early 1960's, important prehistoric finds took place. The discovery of Late Neolithic cultures in the Rhine and Meuse delta area was named after Vlaardingen: the Vlaardingen Culture. They have been dated at between 2700-2000 B.C.

The city itself has various historical and artistic monuments, although from a much more recent time period. Golden memories of golden ages.

Vlaardingen attained city status at the time of Count Floris V.

Although Vlaardingen is no longer an important seaport, it still seems as if nothing has changed since the days when small-scale navigation was the way of life here. It was the same for the port of Maassluis. Ocean tugs and salvors played major roles in this city's history. This port serves as home station for the ships of the State Pilotage Service and headquarters for a salvage company. This is the perfect place for a museum devoted to river and ocean towage. The white building with the tower on top is that National Sleepvaartmuseum.
It keeps the memory alive of Jan de Hartog's Hollands Glorie. The steam tug boat "Furie" moored in front of the museum, actually did appear in the TV series "Hollands Glorie".

Maassluis prides itself on being the first port on the Nieuwe Waterweg; that is, on the northern bank. Being the home port of the towing service, it was the obvious place to situate the museum. The old steam-tug "Furie" is the open-air attraction of this museum.

Hoek van Holland

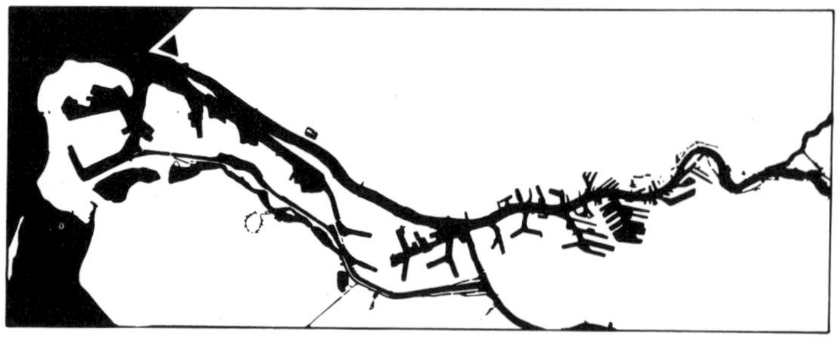

Harbour mouth Hoek van Holland, an extraordinary example of hydraulic engineering.
Some figures:
6,5 million t. of fine gravel,
1,5 million t. of coarse gravel
80 million cubic metres of sand
5,5 million t. rubble
60,000 large concrete blocks
70,000 small concrete blocks

The first leg of our photo-safari has brought us full circle to the concrete block dams near Hoek van Holland.
As techniques in navigation and industrialization have become more highly developed, Rotterdam was forced to modernize the mouth of the harbour, since the existing harbour agglomeration had reached the limit of its capacity. Since the tendency was toward more economical modes of shipping, increasingly larger sizes of ships were being used for mass transport. This, in turn, influenced the modernization of the harbour mouth.
These dams only needed to be as large as was necessary for the flow of water, navigation and reduction of the wave activity. Thus the crown was limited to 2 meters above sea level, by 8 meters wide. Huge amounts of material were used in the construction of these dams. The design of this harbour mouth allowed for ships with a 53 ft. (16.15 meters) draught up to 62 ft. (19.28 meters). This renovation at Hoek van Holland is a great credit to Dutch hydraulic engineers of that time: Adriaan Volker, from Rotterdam, Van Hattum and Blankevoort from Beverwijk and Bos & Kalis from Papendrecht.

WATERWAYS

Hollandsche IJssel

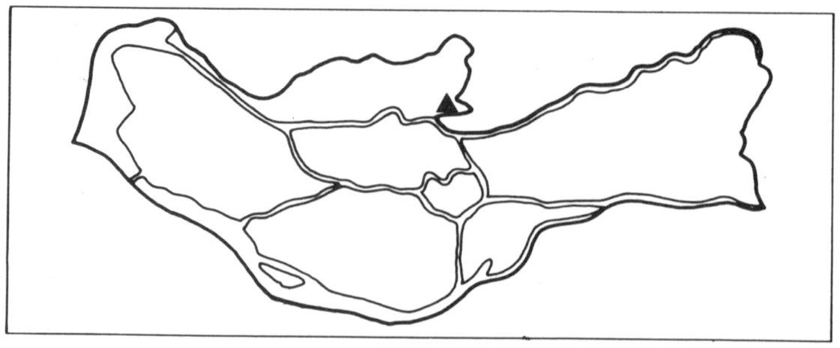

Stemming the floods was one of the very first enterprises to be carried out when the Delta works started after the flooding of 1953. Should the old dykes along the Hollandse IJssel have given way, the whole of South Holland as far as Leiden would have been inundated.

The date is 31 January 1953. The wind is blowing threateningly in a northwesterly direction. In a powerful 1,000 km wide sweep, water poured out of the North Sea in the direction of the southern coast of The Netherlands. It was spring tide! Then it happened. Dikes were crushed. That night 300,000 people lost all they had. The desperate cry: "That kind of disaster... never again!" led to the adoption of the Delta Law. It offered a framework, the exact details of which, still had to be worked out.
8 May 1958 saw the completion of the movable storm-surge barrier in the Hollandse IJssel near Krimpen a/d IJssel. During future storms, the heart of the Randstad – a name given to the western region of the Netherlands, encompassing the largest cities – would thus be better protected than by the IJssel dikes, which are built on very weak ground. The actual concept of the Delta Plan dates back much further.
In 1937, the Public Works Department was already studying the possibilities of flood protection, when unusually high water levels threaten, as they do once every few centuries. Therefore in January of 1953 the Delta Commission was able to put to use its years of study and preparation.

52

Nieuwe Maas

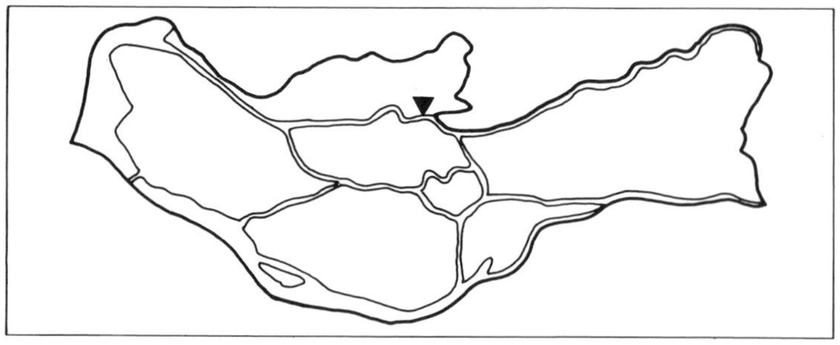

The enormous watertower near the Maas esplanade, which formerly provided the pressure for the domestic water supply. Now that the technique of water supply has changed, an alternative use has been found for the tower – that of housing.

Water is the most curious natural resource on this earth. It has been prayed to, blessed and cursed. It's been fought about and fought against. Entire civilizations became extinct as their water sources dried up or were not used to their best advantage.
Water is found everywhere. Still its chemical formula, H_2O, remains unchanged. Water is necessary for life itself. Yet man is not always satisfied to leave the water in its natural surroundings.
Where fresh water is not found naturally, new sources must be broached. Rotterdam draws its water from the Amer River, below the Biesbos and purifies it for drinking. One of the places in which this takes place is the Kralingen Water Treatment Plant near the Van Brienenoord bridge – a good example of modern architecture.
Next to the Kralingen Water Treatment Plant on the other side of the northern entrance ramp to the Van Brienenoord bridge, construction of a gigantic waste-water purification plant is underway. One could literally say that clean and dirty water lie in each others paths.

The production plant Kralingen is an example of modern architecture. But water is still the issue.
On the other side of the Brienen-oordbrug a large wastewater purification installation is being built.

Lek

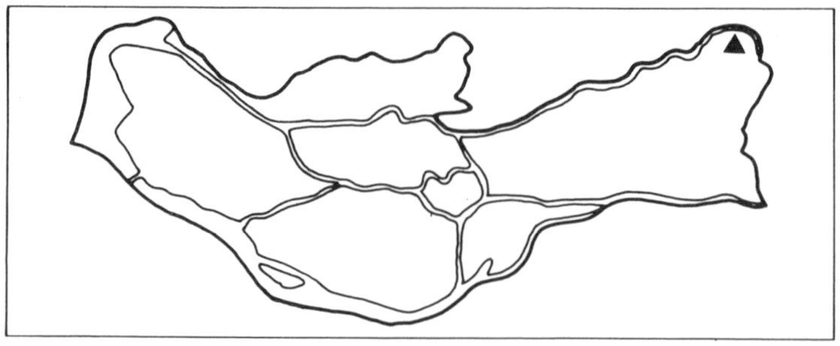

The flood barriers in the Lek near Hagestein, and the barrage upstream in the Nederrijn near Driel, are needed to regulate the waterlevel. The regulation of the traffic flow over the river is much more difficult.

Far and wide before us, stretches the land which the poets sung, as the silver belt of The Netherlands. Man and water, as both friend and enemy, conspired to paint this picture. In earlier years, the rivers could only be kept in check by dikes, yet they were never able to be completely tamed. Skillful engineers have developed strategically located dams, which nowadays regulate the water level. Good examples of this are found at Driel in the Lower Rhine (Neder Rijn) and near Hagestein in the Lek River. Both dams are important switches in regulating the water level of the major rivers. Hagestein, with its white towers, serves as a contrasting accent to the surrounding greenery. The towns of Everdingen, Goilberdingen and Culemborg can be seen on the horizon, coming out from under a blanket of fog. These are the bounds which we do not plan to overstep on this photo-safari. The Lek Bridge (Lekbrug) rises majestically out of the placid riverland. At that time it took over the heavy traffic flow from the former Lekbrug and highway route A2. And now it is the highway route A27, the direct connection between the South and the North of the Netherlands through the Flevo polders which helps to unburden the Lekbrug. On this highway the bridge near Houten falls right in between these two photographs.

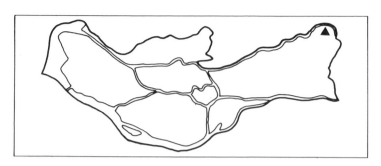

Nieuwe Maas

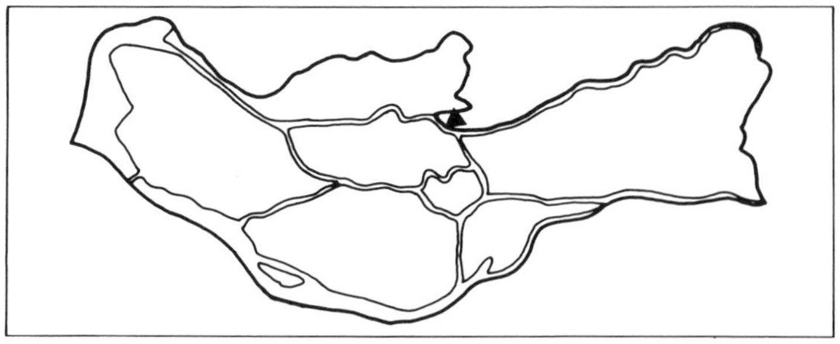

From the Brienenoordbrug we can see, to the north, the large precincts of the Van der Giessen de Noord yards. They seem to be scattered in an even line along the Nieuwe Maas like building blocks.

Judging by its name, things can be pretty restless in the Storm Polder in the fathest western section of Krimpenerwaard, the industrial centre of the community, Krimpen aan den IJssel. Several companies of economic importance to The Netherlands are located here, such as van der Giessen-de Noord N.V., a major shipbuilding enterprise. This company can be seen from far away, with its gigantic shipbuilding hall. In this ''construction palace'' one of the largest (if not THE largest) industrial halls in Western Europe, free from the influence of weather conditions and thus an optimal working environment, shipbuilding schedules can be considerably shortened. This is an important factor among the stiff, world-wide competition. Van der Giessen-de Noord considers itself an important part of the group of large ship yards in the European Common Market.
The bulk of the company's work consists of the building of new ships, and navy vessels, ship repair and plastics.
The greatest strength the Storm Polder has, which makes a man feel very small, is its powerful demonstration of trust in the future.

Unfortunately, for the time being, good news is scarce in the world of ship building. For years now, shipbuilding and ship repair have been a cause of great distress to the Dutch economy. But a leading world port can't do without either one of them.
Although the problems in the national and international world of shipbuilding are far from being eliminated, and although economic storms beat down on the sky-high roof of their ultramodern construction hall in the Storm Polder, new working regulations and cleverly-designed production methods enable van der Giessen-de Noord to come out fighting. Adaptable organisation, precise planning, reorganization processes, unanimous goal-orientation and determination are the demands which must be met by all, who want to keep putting food on their table.

It is only once inside these buildings that one becomes aware of their immensity. Their size is so enormous that one feels very insignificant. Despite the activity, the recession in shipbuilding is a serious threat.

Waal, Merwede

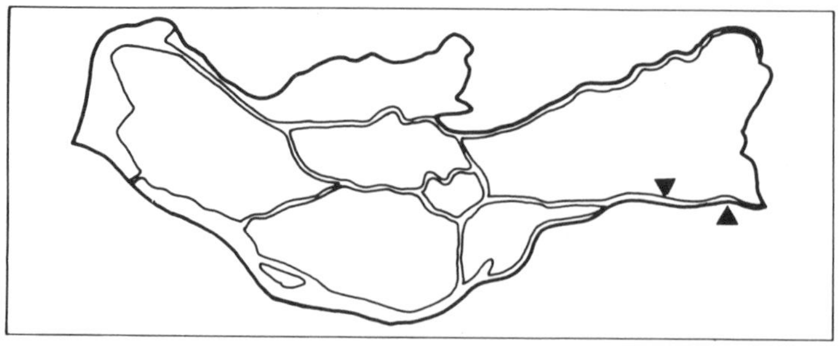

Sometimes the Dutch are very obstinate in making a difference between the conventional spelling and the pronounciation of the names of towns and villages. Take for instance this fortified town, situated where the Linge flows into the Merwede. It is spelt: Gorinchem and it is pronounced: Gorkum.

The name of this town has several different spellings. Take your pick: Gorinchem, Gorcum or Gorkum. Using Gorkum as a starting point, you can choose any direction: to Rijnmond or the Ruhr area, south to Breda and Antwerp and to Utrecht and other northern destinations. The highway routes A15 and A27 intersect at Gorkum. The cross-country rail line from Dordrecht to Nijmegen also goes through Gorkum. This city, located in the south eastern corner of South Holland is a noteworthy industry and trade centre. It serves as the commercial, cultural and social centre for the area. Gorkum attracts residents of the surrounding riverland and of the Land of Altena and Heusden on the opposite side of the Boven Merwede River.

Gorkum is a picturesque city, with old churches and other historical buildings. The view of the rivier, bustling with activity, remains an exciting spectacle. Originating in the Betuwe, the 108 km long Linge River, flowing by way of the Merwede Kanaal near Gorkum, entrusts itself to the care of the Boven Merwede River.

A visit to Gorkum is quite revealing.

Within view of "where Meuse and Waal flow together" as once colorfully described by the poet Tollens, in the North West of the Bommelerwaard, lies Loevestein Castle. It was built by the rather daring Dirk Loef van Horne. In 1357 this gentleman supposedly borrowed money from Count Willem V of Holland using Altena as collateral. This story continues to impress each new generation which hears it.
In 1614 Loevestein became a state prison. One of the first prisoners there was Hugo the Great. Imprisoned in 1619, two years later he managed to escape in a bookcase. In the 19th century this castle was fitted up as a military fort. It is situated in the surroundings of the New Netherlands Water line, which as recently as 1939/1940 was made ready for defense purpose. Although Loevestein may be a tourist attraction, it was and still is a sombre, menacing castle, built for the purpose of ruling the world and when neccessary, to make mincemeat of the enemy.
During wintertime or springtime, if the river floods the surrounding land, Loevestein rises above it all as one solid obstinate block. Loevestein is meant to be taken seriously!

In the North West of the Bommelerwaard where the two rivers, Maas en Waal, flow together – as once described by the poet Tollens – lies Loevestein, a medieval castle. Hugo de Groot's escape in a bookcase in 1621 gave it its fame.

Merwede, Noord, Oude Maas

On this triple waterway, the Merwede, the Noord and the Oude Maas we see Papendrecht at the top of the righthand side and Zwijndrecht on the left. At the botton on the left, not visible on the large photograph, lies Grootint, winner of the 1983 Steel award for the construction of the Willemsbrug.

On the southeastern tip of IJsselmonde, along the Old Meuse River (Oude Maas) and the North River (Noord) lies Zwijndrecht. In the Groote Lindt industrial park several important companies have set up shop. One of them is the internationally-known Grootint BV, which has made a name for itself in the steel industry. This concern includes several subsidiaries.
The Board Members of the Steel Construction Branch Group awarded Grootint BV the National Steel Industry Prize of 1983, in the category ''Bridges'' for its construction of the Willemsbrug in Rotterdam.
In the opinion of the jury, this bridge stands out because of the way steel was used in its construction: effectively, economically and aesthetically. Recently, on the Grootint yard, 2 large assembly plants and a workshop for pipe bending and fabrication started production.

Noord, Lek, Nieuwe Maas

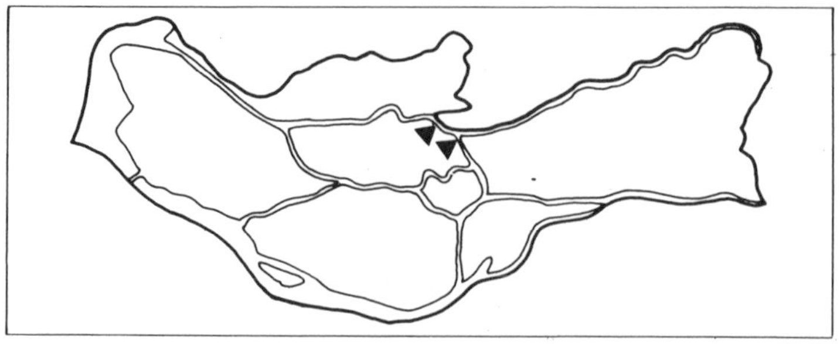

The upper course of the Noord, seen from the traffic bridge at the crossing of the Noord, Lek, and Nieuwe Maas. Krimpen aan de Lek lies above, Kinderdijk to the right, Ridderkerk and Slikkerveer to the left. Further on we see Bolnes, where the Boele company has experienced the recession that has also affected the ship repair industry.

In Slikkerveer, shipbuilder Pieter Boele and carpenter Cornelis Boele tried their luck on a 10 x 20 meter shipyard. Pieter Boele (1827-1887) is considered to be the founder of the company which has gained international fame as Boele Scheepswerven en Machine fabriek.
Little is known about the ships built in those early years but since 1872, records were kept of all building orders. When industrialization took place along the Rhine and Ruhr Rivers, activating the market for the transportation of raw materials from Rotterdam to Germany, there was great demand for new Rhine vessels. Boele took advantage of there developments. Due to land purchases for the purpose of expansion of their site, the business moved up to Bolnes. An engineering works was acquired and before long the manufacture of steam engines was going strong. When, in 1915, Boele's company took its present name, it also began building seagoing vessels.
For the municipality of Ridderkerk, Boele's Scheepswerven en Machinefabriek is of great importance in the social sector and for local employment.
Currently, national and international ship building is struggling to keep afloat, which inevitably effects Boele as well.

Biesbosch, Hollandsch Diep, Hellegat

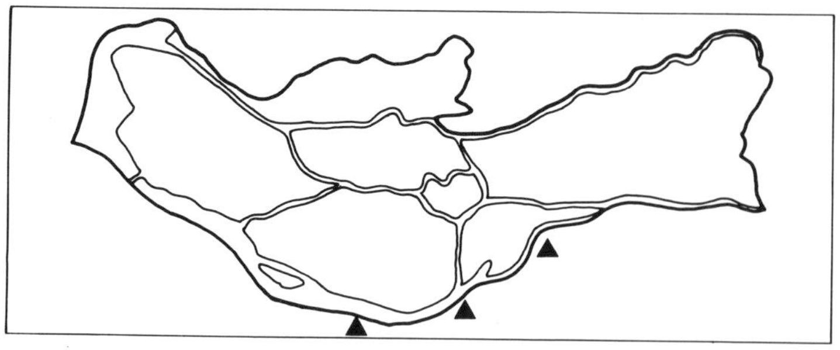

De Biesbos is a maze of rivers and rivulets which are a result of the great flood of 1421, the St. Elisabeth flood, when the Zuidhollandse Waard was entirely engulfed. As a result of the Delta works there are no longer tidal streams.

Man is obliged to leave the basic natural elements of his environment the way they originally were. In this regard, the quality of the world's water supply is a chronic headache.
The Water Companies of Rotterdam, Dordrecht and Brabant have huge reservoirs in the Biesbos, which are large enough to allow plenty of time for self-cleaning of the water from the Maas River. Injections of air, useful in the purification process, provide noticeable improvement in the quality of the drinking water. Altogether, the reservoirs can hold at least 80 million cubic meters. After the natural purification process, the water is pumped to the Water Companies' purification installations for final treatment. Only after the completion of this phase, is the water suitable for drinking.
The Maas is a rain river and during dry summers occasionally runs rather low. However, drinking water supplies must not be endangered under any circumstances. Thus, these reservoirs contain reserves which can be used when the river is low.

The highway-bridge, dating from 1936, which spans the Hollands Diep near Moerdijk was adapted to fit the growing traffic flow in the 1970s. The older skillfully-crafted parts of the bridge were removed, making room for new parts twice as wide as the old ones. The old pillars have remained.
The former expressions "above the Moerdijk" and "below the Moerdijk" are no longer widely used. They date from the time when the Hollands Diep River formed a hurdle in the North to South bound traffic.
Who could forget the names of Johan Willem Friso, stadholder in Friesland and the Prince of the House of Orange, who unfortunately drowned near the Moerdijk in 1711?
Within the framework of the Delta Works, new highway junctions were built, such as Hellegatsplein – a triangle at the point where Brabant, the Hoekse Waard and Goeree-Overflakkee meet.
On sunny holidays and Sundays, this junction in the scene of record-breaking traffic jams.

For many years the Moerdijkbrug was a symbol of the differences between the north and south of the country. New connections, such as the Hellegatsplein connection (also a part of the Delta works) diminish these differences.

Haringvliet

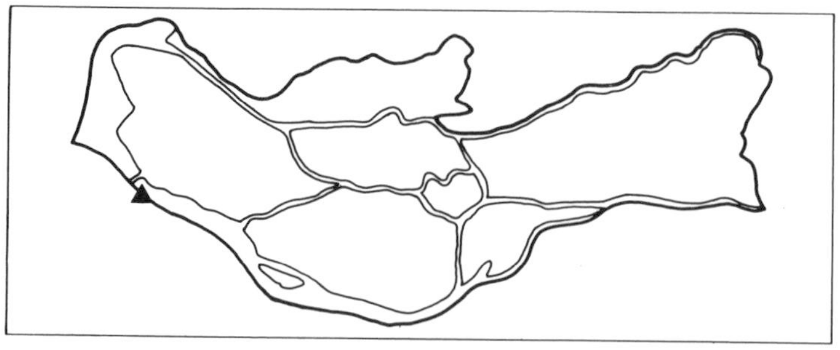

The flattest countryside of The Netherlands, linked by impressive bridges and huge dams, yet separated by inland waterways, is a paradise for the experienced yachtsman. The Grevelingen seen from a different perspective.

At one time, spring tide and storms were plentiful where now many enjoy boating. But you have to know what you are doing.
These closed-off estuaries are not always peaceful. There are several spots where the traces of former disasters are clearly visible.
For the densely populated Randstad this serves as a large recreational area. Free of dangerous tidal currents, it is ideal for all types of water sports.

Although it was a disaster which triggered the Delta Plan, now that the project is nearing completion (the last stages of the building of the storm-surge barrier in the Eastern Scheldt are now underway) this work of art has yielded countless advantages.
The Delta Works are of great importance especially in economizing the fresh water supply in the Netherlands. The damming off of the Volkerak and Haringvliet prevents the fresh water of the Rhine and Meuse Rivers from flowing directly to the sea.

Visible in the foreground, high over Rijnmond, is the Haringvliet, with its locks between Voorne on one side and Goeree on the other. In the background, outside Rijnmond, is the Zealand delta: the Grevelingen lake and the Brouwersdam. Schouwen en Walcheren fade away beyond the horizon.

Oude Maas

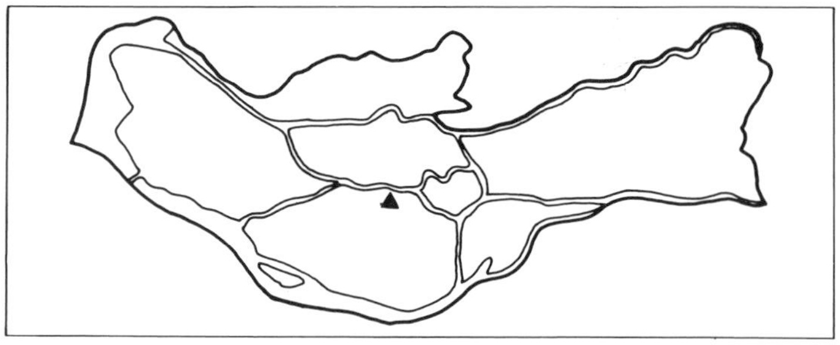

The Oude Maas has become an even more important waterway since the construction of Europoort and the Hartel Kanaal and since the Maas Plain became a centre of industry.
The tugs move quickly and safely round Rotterdam to the Hinterland.

The Old Meuse River (Oude Maas): it's name tells its story. For centuries this was the mouth of the Meuse River and the most important shipping route to Dordrecht. Even now it is still a heavily-travelled river, an important stretch connecting the sea to the hinterland. Barges, especially, make avid use of this route. The unfortunate result of the thousands-of-horsepower -strong motors, creating waves and currents, is the damage they cause to the river banks, Construction of protective dams is an effort to slow down this erosion, as much as possible.
The Oude Maas (now without stagnating locks) has an open connection to Europoort and Maasvlakte, through the Hartelkanaal. The Green tidal river contributes to the land on the outside of the dikes, vital substances for animal and plant life. Twice in every 24-hour period, sections of this land are flooded by surging water.
By damming off the Haringvliet, the tidal rhythm was altered.
The flood mark was lowered and the low water mark was raised.
The landscape of the river banks has remained breathtaking with its osiers, underwood and reedy marsh collar, making it an ideal winter shelter for various types of aquatic birds.

RIVERLANDS AND ISLANDS

Krimpenerwaard

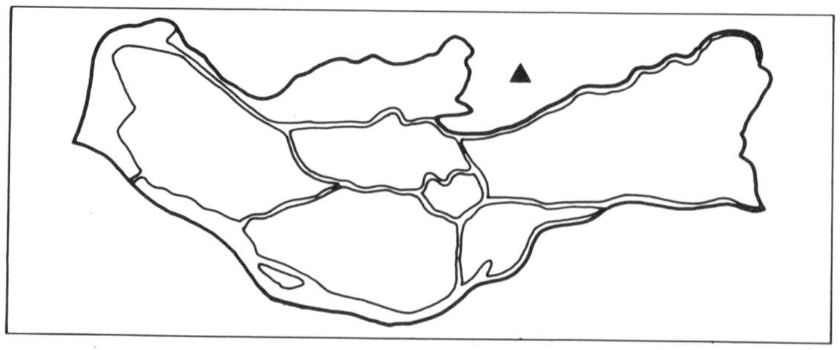

Geographically the Krimpenerwaard is part of the green heart of the Netherlands. ''Waard'' means riverland, and the rivers here are the Hollandse IJssel, the Lek and the Vliet.
A region for grassland birds, with originally poor or ''blue'' pastures.

''Waard'' actually means riverland. Indeed, the Krimpenerwaard is surrounded by three rivers: the Hollandse IJssel, the Lek and the Vlist. Geographically speaking, the Krimpenerwaard is located in ''The Green Belt'' in the central part of the Netherlands. This location makes it one of the most beautiful Dutch riverlands. It is open, flat, low-lying countryside, encircled with dikes, which protect the riverland from the rising water. The pools of water found in many of the diked-in areas is evidence that this attempted protection has failed in the past. These pools, the silent surviving witnesses to disasterous adversity, have become spots of unparalleled beauty.
The Krimpenerwaard is of unequalled value for its landscape and as a nature reserve. A region whose average water level in the rivers is higher than that of the surrounding riverland, it is an ideal spot for grassland birds.
Due to the increased practice of pig-farming which took place in the second half of the 19th century, this formerly poor or ''bluegrass'' land was luckily (or unluckily?) converted into choice hay fields and meadow land for grazing. Near the old duck traps in Berkenwoude are still some protected areas of bluegrass land.

Since 1425, Krimpenerwaard is run by a self-governing polder management committee.
This vast polder countryside, in all of its simpliciity, is equally attractive during all four seasons of the year.
Unfortunately the land is being threatened by advancing housing estates bringing with them the usual disadvantages. The Krimpenerwaard is a most precious ''possession'' for the Dutch and must be guarded with the utmost of care.
Even when winter tightens her icy grip on the riverland, this area loses none of its charm. As thatch-covered farm houses shiver under roofs, grown curved with age and pollard-willow trees pout alongside of frozen watercourses, it might be that we have captured this land at its very best.

Berkenwoude still has a few blue pastures left which are protected, but, due to pig-farming, the rest have been converted into excellent grazing land. The rapidly encroaching housing estates seem far away in this still, wintery landscape of Berkenwoude.

Alblasserwaard

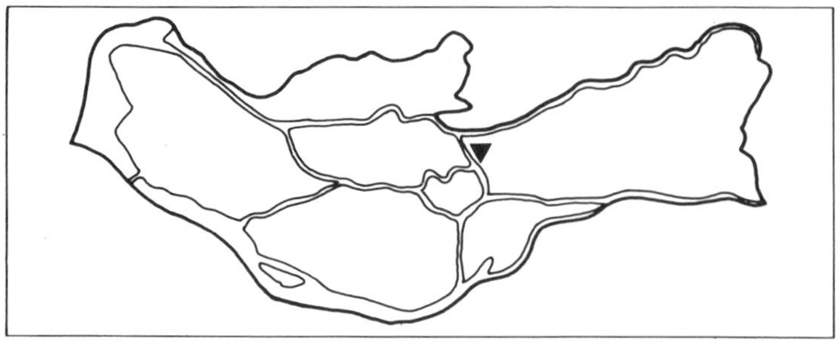

The mills of Kinderdijk, symbolic of Holland. Nowhere else can a more complete group of nineteen mills be found. Small wonder that half the world's tourists must have seen these.

"The wind blows where it will. You hear the sound it makes but you do not know where it comes from, or where it goes." (John 3 : 8) No one would agree with these words more than the miller, who sets the sails toward the wind. The true windmill fan has found his niche when he comes to this fascinating group of windmills at Kinderdijk in the Alblasserwaard. Altogether there are 19 huge mills! Of nostalgic design and built with native bricks and reeds, they are a sight to behold. The beauty of the windmill is in its simple yet practical design. These mills bring us back to nature and its most powerful forces: wind and water.

When the arms of mills are standing still, they serve as signals to neighboring millers. The arms of the mill in the foreground signal joy. The advancing arm has been stopped just before reaching the highest point.

Hoeksche Waard

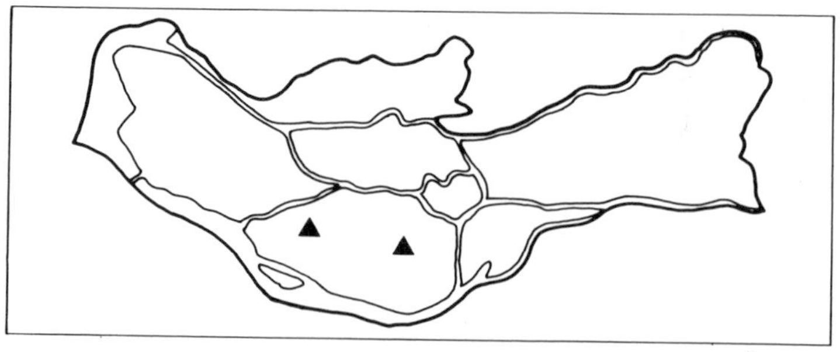

Hoekse Waard has a multiplicity of agricultural enterprises. Formerly it was an arable farming area, but nowadays there is also a great deal of cattle breeding and fruit growing. This picture shows these three elements combined.

The Hoekse Waard is an area of land completely surrounded by rivers. The rivers: Dordtse Kil, Oude Maas, Spui, Vuile Gat, Haringvliet and Hollands Diep create the island. The western part of the waard is called Beijerland.
In the Middle Ages, the eastern section belonged to the Grote Zuid-Hollandse Waard (the Greater South Holland Riverland), which was inundated by the Saint Elizabeth Flood in 1421. Later, by building dikes at Goudswaard and Piershil and aided by the land reclamation of 1581, the Beijerlandse Polder was created. The Count of Egmont named it in honour of his wife, Sabina van Beieren (Bavaria).

The meandering Inland Meuse River (Binnenmaas) is of great importance to the landscape and natural sciences. Beautifully tree-lined dikes, found in the St. Anthony Polder and the surroundings of Munnikenland hem in the stagnant Westmaas tributary. No wonder the Binnenmaas is popular with water sport enthousiasts. The former core of the Hoekse Waard is an ideal family recreation spot. The Heinenoord tunnel to the north, Hellegatsplein to the south and the National Highway route A25 which cuts right through the Hoekse Waard, make the area easily accessible from the Randstad and Brabant.

Of course, the pressure of Greater Rotterdam on this rural area is heavy, although it is not so much an industrial pressure as the growth of recreation. Here in De Luie Man (The Lazy Man) the lazy man of Rotterdam may enjoy himself.

Voorne-Putten

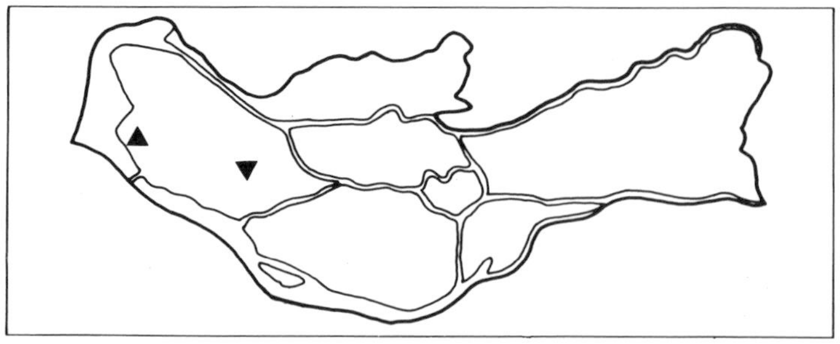

Voorne is separated from Putte by the Bernisse, an old river-branch which meanders along the villages Zuidland, Abbenbroek and Heenvliet to the Brielse Maas.
An eldorado for lovers of scenic beauty!

On the southeastern side of the lake, Voornse Meer, pushed aside by Maasvlakte, the original coast of Voorne can be found.
This southern portion has had a constant struggle with the sea, against which protective measures had to be taken. The beach was widened out father to the north, forming new dunes there.
This is how valleys and a dune lake, het Brede Water, came to be.
There are foot paths and even a few ''outlook dunes''.
The dune landscape is characterized by interesting overgrowth.
In the central dunes, there is alternating overgrowth and dry grass-land.

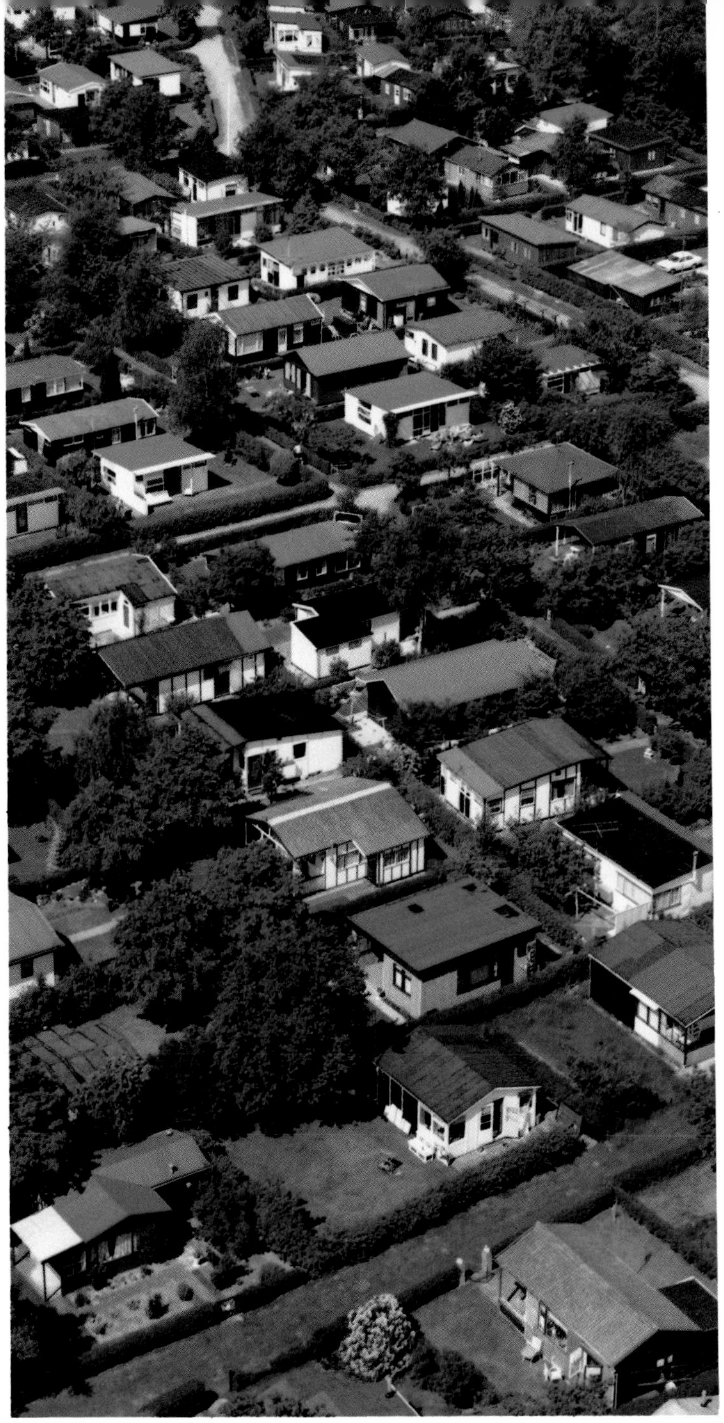

The coastal strip of Voorne offers a surprising variety of recreational possibilities year round. The dunes are internationally famous for their rich assortment of plant and animal life.
To stroll along the beach here, through the dunes is to set out on an adventure.
The magnificient coastal area with its well-known sea-side resorts of Rockanje and Oostvoorne draws thousands of bathers a year. This is not surprising since the spacious beach is 10 kilometers long and 100 meters wide.
As a result of the ongoing battle against the sea, the dune area was closed off in the latter part of the Middle Ages.
Rather unfortunately, the Delta Works have left their mark on the coast, robbing it of much of its flora and fauna. Being a recreational area does not help matters either. Yet, beneath the clouds of Europoort and Maasvlakte, Voorne's coast remains a paradise for the people of Rijnmond, whose hearts it has captured.
The hundreds of vacation cottages and extensive facilities for day-trippers just go to show how important a part Voorne's coast plays in satisfying the recreational needs of the area.

The border on the other side of Voorne is formed by the dunes. Here is much natural beauty as well, but possibly fewer people to appreciate it. 'Passive recreation' it is called by some officials, somewhat condescendingly. But who may decide what the exhausted city-dweller needs for recreation, if not he himself?

IJsselmonde

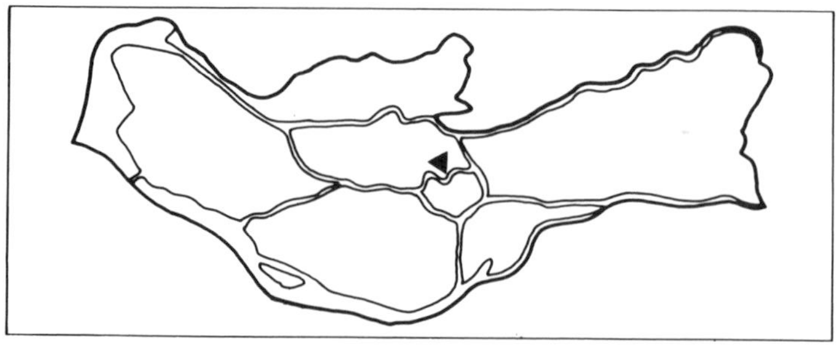

The Waal (a disused tributary) meanders peacefully along Rijsoord on its way to Heerjansdam. Rijsoord, a village in an area where flaxgrowing was once of great importance, is now the garden of the municipality of Ridderkerk. As seen here, it is more than just a maze of motorways with traffic jams.

Rijsoord, a village where flax-growing was once of great importance, is now the garden of the nearby municipality of Ridderkerk.
"A town worth being stuck in a traffic jam for", to quote the Mayor. Hemmed in by a maze of highways, each with unbelievable numbers of lanes, and the Waal (a stagnant tributary), Rijsoord is nevertheless a truly peaceful oasis.
"Het Waaltje", as the tributary is familiarly called, winds romantically from Hendrik-Ido-Ambacht through Rijsoord, on its way to Heerjansdam.

The summertime sees a colourful picture of small-scale watersports taking place. During wintertime, when the water freezes, it becomes a skaters' paradise while in the in-between times, it is a haven for fishermen. They come from far and wide, each to their own fixed spot.
Here in Rijsoord, is convincing evidence that Rijnmond is more than a world port.

CITIES AND TOWNS

Schoonhoven, Lekkerkerk

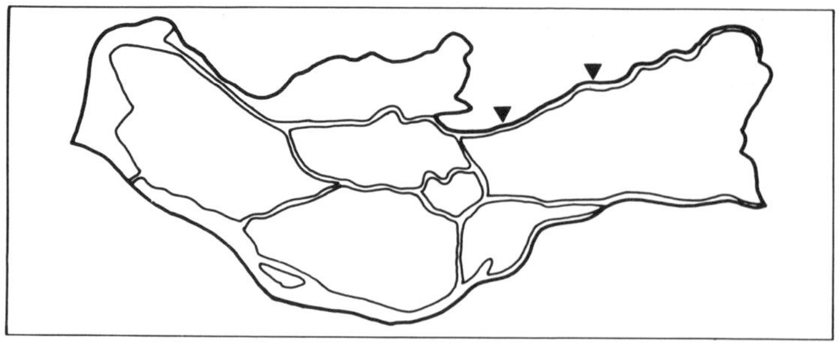

Schoonhoven, the town on the Vlist in the Krimpenerwaard and on the border between Zuid-Holland and Utrecht, is famous for its silver. Since the fourteenth century Schoonhoven has been a synonym for silver-smithing. Little wonder that the government trade school for silver- and gold-smithing is situated here.

Schoonhoven lies in the heart of the riverland, centrally situated with respect to the Krimpenerwaard, Alblasserwaard and Lopikerwaard. The town on the Lek River – the town of silversmiths, was once also the town of carpet weavers. Encircled by 17th century walls, Schoonhoven guards several historical and cultural monuments. The Great or St. Bartholomeus Church was recorded in the Citizens Annals of 1364. Originally a cruciform church, and in the 17th century rebuilt in the style of the Doric order, this church finally acquired its present form in our century. Effective restoration has put an end to the sagging tower which had been 1½ meters out of alignment. The fact that the church took on a slanted countenance never seemed to bother its admirers.

Of international fame is the silver trade, dating back to the Middle Ages. The former barracks on the Oude Haven house The Netherlands' Gold, Silver and Clock Museum.

Schoonhoven, situated at the mouth of the romantic Vlist River, is also noteworthy for its architectural beauty. However fascinating her past may be, or whatever interesting scenery she boasts, the town is much more than an Open Air Museum.

Modern industries such as pottery, wood working and foodstuffs offer Schoonhoven the potential to continue for some years to come.

Amidst the greenery and unspoiled land of the Krimpenerwaard lies the community of Lekkerkerk, west of Schoonhoven. The municipality includes the villages of Opperduit and Schuwacht and their surroundings in addition to Lekkerkerk. Many of the villages do not appear on any map.
At one time, Lekkerkerk was a part of the Lek manor, which also included Krimpen and Ridderkerk. By way of his marriage, Count Engelbrecht I of Nassau-Dillenberg acquired this manor. Thus the ties of Lekkerkerk, Krimpen and Ridderkerk with the Nassaus, are very old ones.

The St. Elizabeth's Flood of 1421 ''endowed'' Lekkerkerk with a small pool of water. This soothed the pain of the flood by enabling the area to become a nature reserve: Bakkerswaal, which boasts an old duck trap.
In the early 1980s, Lekkerkerk became the talk of the town due to the upsetting discovery of serious soil contamination. The soil in the area involved was dug up, 4 meters deep, and filled with clean sand.
The wood and metal industries, shipbuilding and construction companies keep Lekkerkerk's river banks lively.

Lekkerkerk aquired a sad reputation in the recent past as being the community with the first pollution scandal. Since then there have been other poison scandals and will perhaps be others in the future. It is the penalty for an inconsiderate policy in the past. Lekkerkerk was the first community to resolve this.

Ameide, Nieuwpoort

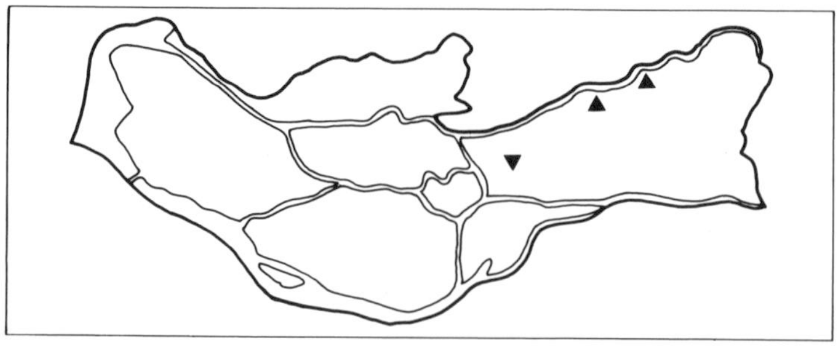

Downstream from the Lek, on the same bank and still in the Alblasserwaard, is Nieuwpoort; a miniature town with municipal rights since 1283.
In former days a war-stricken town, it is now a protected area.

Moving along the Lekdijk away from Lexmond, the row of 18th century houses on Voorstraat meets the eye. Nieuwpoort, almost directly opposite Schoonhoven in the Krimpenerwaard, obtained town rights in 1283. It is situated at the former boundary of Holland and Het Sticht. In turbulent times, quite often Nieuwpoort found itself stuck in the middle of a fighting zone. The years 1482, 1514, 1524 and 1567 are recorded in blood in the Town Annals. The fortifications, which were built at the time of the French invasion in 1672 (the Year of Fear: the government was desperate, the country irretrievable and the people irrational) with their tree-lined walls, bastions and moats, are beautifully well-preserved. The core of the town is a protected area. The famous Battle of Nieuwpoort in 1600, fought and won by Prince Maurits, has nothing to do with this town. It was fought at Nieuwpoort in West-Flanders.
The quaint town hall in Ameide dates from 1644 and has a magnificent 17th century interior. The reformed Church also has attained a ripe old age. Built around 1500, its late-Romanesque tower is from the 13th century.

Ameide, on the south bank, received its municipal rights in the fourteenth century. This is the north-eastern beginning of the Alblasserwaard, one of the oldest polder areas in The Netherlands.

Try to imagine this contrast: on the one side the 20th century harbour and industrial area of Rijnmond and on the other, the countryside of Alblasserwaard: typical old-Dutch polder land. Numerous floods engulfed this low-lying peat-bog down through the centuries, most recently in 1953.
''He who controls the wind and the clouds and plans the way our paths will take'' has left a deep impression on the hearts of the people of Alblasserwaard, who were so dependent on the forces of nature. The dredger and the farmer, the farm labourer and the maid, all murmured about Divine Judgement. This attitude is exemplified in the upright countenance of the homesteads along the river dikes and Graafstroom River, of which Truus Gerhardt writes, in ''The Homesteads'' (''De Hofstede''):
''This is the secluded house, which keeps to itself,
where Holland works and prays as the seasons flow by,
where rigidly-folded hands profess a strong faith
and a orthodox people honours their God with hard work.''

Dordrecht

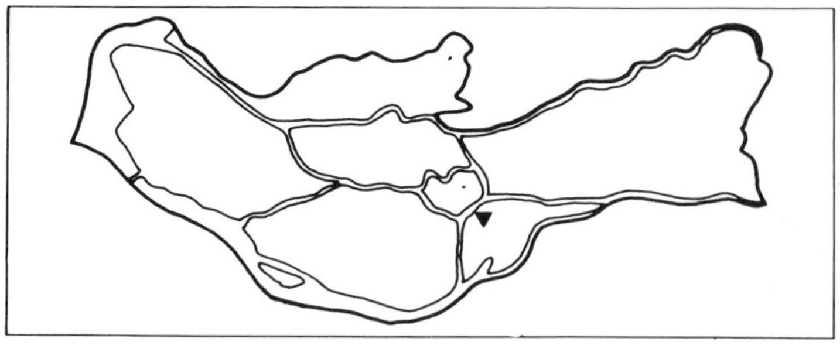

Dordrecht still shows the glory of the past. Once the most important port; whoever wished to sail the Rhine or the Maas had to submit to the laws of Dordrecht. Later, in 1572, it was the first city to have secret and free elections for the states.

Dordrecht, located on the island of Dordrecht, is one of the oldest and most picturesque harbour cities in the country. Lying at the crossroads of heavily-travelled rivers enabled this city to become a centre for trade and industry. In 1220, Count Willem I of Holland officially handed Dordrecht the status of "city".
Numerous buildings recall Dordrecht's rich history, as they take us back through many, many centuries. The Great Church (Grote Kerk) dominates the scene. The building of this church, which was begun in 1080 took centuries. But they who have faith, also have time to wait. Its tower dates back to the 13th century. The nave, transept, choir and choir-gallery are from the late 14th, early 16th century, while the magnificent organ was acquired one hundred years later.
Straight away, at the beginning of the Eighty Years War of independence, Dordrecht chose to side with Prince Willem of Orange. Whether or not this was done in their own interest is left to the imagination.
At any rate, the Sea-Beggars had possession of the river mouths. Dordrecht, in her position of safety, behind the great water, became the headquarters for the revolutionary government. On 19 July 1572, the first free Estates of the towns of Holland met here.

As an inland harbour city, Dordrecht was stiff competition for Rotterdam until about the year 1600. Then, her position gradually weakened. In the 18th century, despite the building of new wharfs, Dordrecht was overshadowed by the Maas City.
When the times changed, Dordrecht changed with them and devoted itself wholeheartedly to industry. This succesful venture continues to be so today. The most important businesses are the metal, chemical and construction industries.
The Drecht tunnel (opened on 15 November 1977 by then Queen Juliana) was of far-reaching importance, not only for the highway route A16 but for the town of Dordrecht as well. The only one of its kind in The Netherlands, the Drecht tunnel has a total of 8 lanes, four going in each direction. This tunnel is part of the total reconstruction of the overburdened A16, THE highway connecting Amsterdam and Paris.
It is an important link between the Rotterdam and Antwerp harbour basins as well. Locally-speaking it gave Dordrecht, Zwijndrecht and Hendrik-Ido-Ambacht the possibility of adjusting and improving their road networks to fit the new situation.

But time has not stood still in Dordrecht. A modern car tunnel with no less than eight traffic lanes leading to Zwijndrecht and Rotterdam shows how intensive its traffic is. During the great flood in 1953 the water reached even as far as here.

Westmaas, Oud-Beijerland

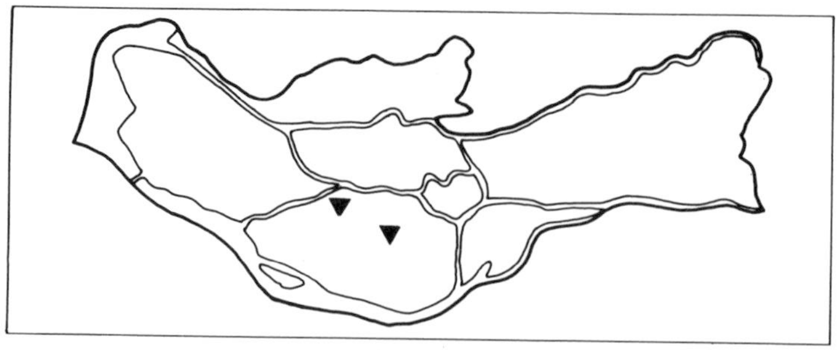

Westmaas, on this side of the Maas, with inland dykes, and Mijnsherenland on the other side, form the heart of the Hoekse Waard. A pleasant area in which to live.

At the head of the dammed-off Maas River lies the friendly village of Westmaas. Located in the old core of the Hoekse Waard, this farming village is becoming more and more suburban. In the center of the village stands an old Reformed Church which was built in 1650. It has been beautifully restored and still has the original pulpit. The renowned Cornelis Elisa van Koetsveld (1807-1893), theologian, writer and court chaplain to King Willem III, onced preached in this church. He is the author of ''Sketches of the Mastland parsonage'' (''Schetsen uit de pastorij van Mastland''). Dr. Koetsveld was referring to the parish of Westmaas, which had been entrusted to his care. The picturesque village has a good view of the water sports which take place on the stagnant tributary, as does Mijnsheerenland, on the other side of the water. There, the house called Hof van Moerkerken, surrounded by a moat, recalls the days when the Rotterdam regents, who used to wear wigs, came here seeking their amusement. The adjoining woodland is a valuable botanical and ornithological paradise.
Westmaas and Mijnsheerenland are well worth a visit by those who relish peace and quiet.

Lamoraal, Count of Egmont, must have been quite taken in by his wife, Sabina van Beieren, when in 1557, he chose her name for the planned polder in the western part of the Hoekse Waard.
Near the Spui River, where quaint little ferry boats make the crossing to Putten, it appears as if time has stood still.
This is something that can't be said about the flourishing community of Oud-Beijerland, though, where many important industries are situated and the people are very enterprising. Oud-Beijerland serves as a regional centre both economically-speaking and in the area of eductation.

The old city centre, which looks as if it were drawn with a ruler, along the perfectly straight canal, contains many historical buildings: the Reformed Church, dating back to 1650, the Town Hall, interestingly enough built over the canal, and various stepped gables.
When it comes to water sports, Oud-Beijerland proudly boasts a snug inland harbour, which offers a warm welcome to boaters.

Oud-Beijerland has a central function for the Hoekse Waard. But it is clear that it is an historical centre as well. In the future it may be connected to the Benelux tunnel, but for the time being we have to make a detour or make use of the ferry to cross the Spui to...

Hellevoetsluis

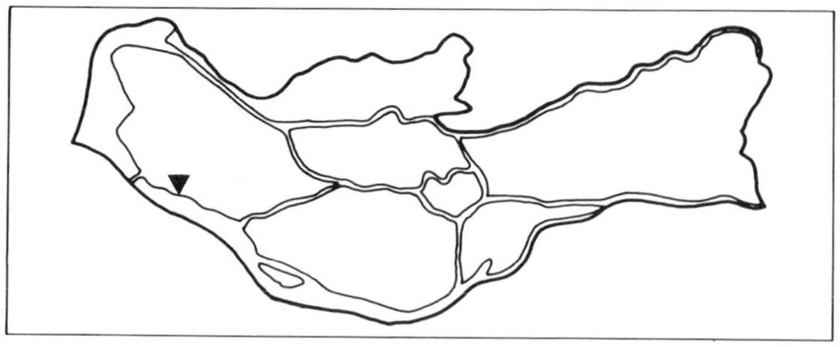

From Oud-Beijerland in the Hoekse Waard to Hellevoetsluis is a short jaunt if you take the Spui. This fortified town, with its clearly visible ramparts, boasts of a glorious maritime past. Stadtholder William III sailed from here with a fleet of over 400 ships to become King of England in 1688.

Hellevoetsluis is rich in history. This fortified city, with its clearly visible ramparts, boasts of a glorious maritime past.
Piet Hein and Michiel de Ruyter, 17th century Dutch naval officers, once encamped here.
In 1688 nobleman Willem III sailed from Hellevoetsluis with a fleet of 400 ships to England to become its King.
Now Hellevoetsluis is a first-rate watersport centre which attracts not only its own ''Hellevoeters'' but other inhabitants of Rijnmond, as well.

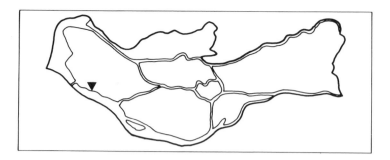

In 1975 Hellevoetsluis was designated as the core of an expansion project whose purpose would be to provide housing for those who work in Europoort and Maasvlakte. To meet this goal, to the east of the Voornse Kanaal new housing areas were built. Despite the large-scale building of entire cities which was taking place, by constructing lower buildings and by beautifully landscaping the fast-growing new urban areas, the result has been a very pleasant place to live. These are the reasons that Hellevoetsluis is a many-faceted city: a residential city, only 15 km from Rijnmond with a wide variety of recreational possibillities, a city surrounded by water and a city in full bloom.

In the last century the Voorns Kanaal gave new impetus to Hellevoetsluis. But when the Nieuwe Waterweg came into being the importance of the former canal diminished. Only the Navy remained there, and has since departed, but the old concrete dock remains. Beyond the canal building development is under way.

Brielle

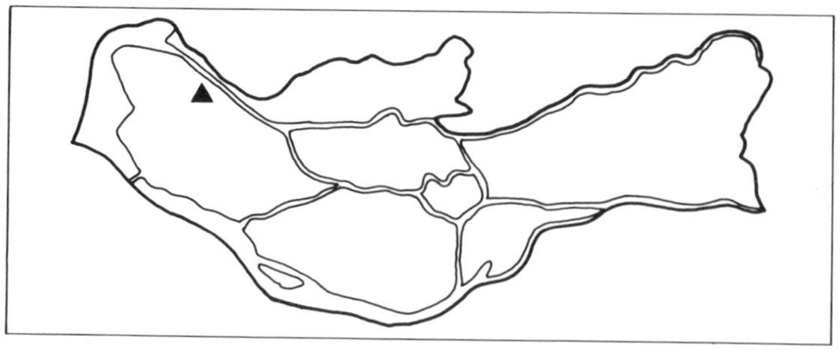

Brielle, a resting-point in the rapidly-changing Rijnmond area. This picture shows, from top to bottom: the city extension in the south, the historial settlement with nine bastions and five ravelins, the Brielse Maas, the Hartelkanaal, the Petroleum Port, the Nieuwe Waterweg and Maassluis.

Brielle, sometimes known as Den Briel, on the former island of Voorne has changed drastically since its early days. A different ''gate'' than the one in the song, ''In the name of Orange, open the gate'', has made it possible for this fortress-town to be encircled by a most unique landscape: Europoort.

The town has preserved many memories of its turbulent, yet rich past. The walls, with their bastions and ramparts, are basically intact. Although only the foundation remains of the North Gate (the Beggars Gate), the newer Quay and Long Gates (Kaai- and Langepoort) are still part of the town's image. Old merchants' houses with handsome gables remind us of the wealth and importance of this town in earlier days. At that time, fishing was a major source of income. But Brielle saw its days as a harbour town quickly slipping away, when such projects were undertaken as the silting up of the Maas, the dredging of the Voorns Kanaal and later, the Nieuwe Waterweg.

The majority of Brielle's commuters work for companies in the harbours of Maasvlakte, Europoort and Botlek.

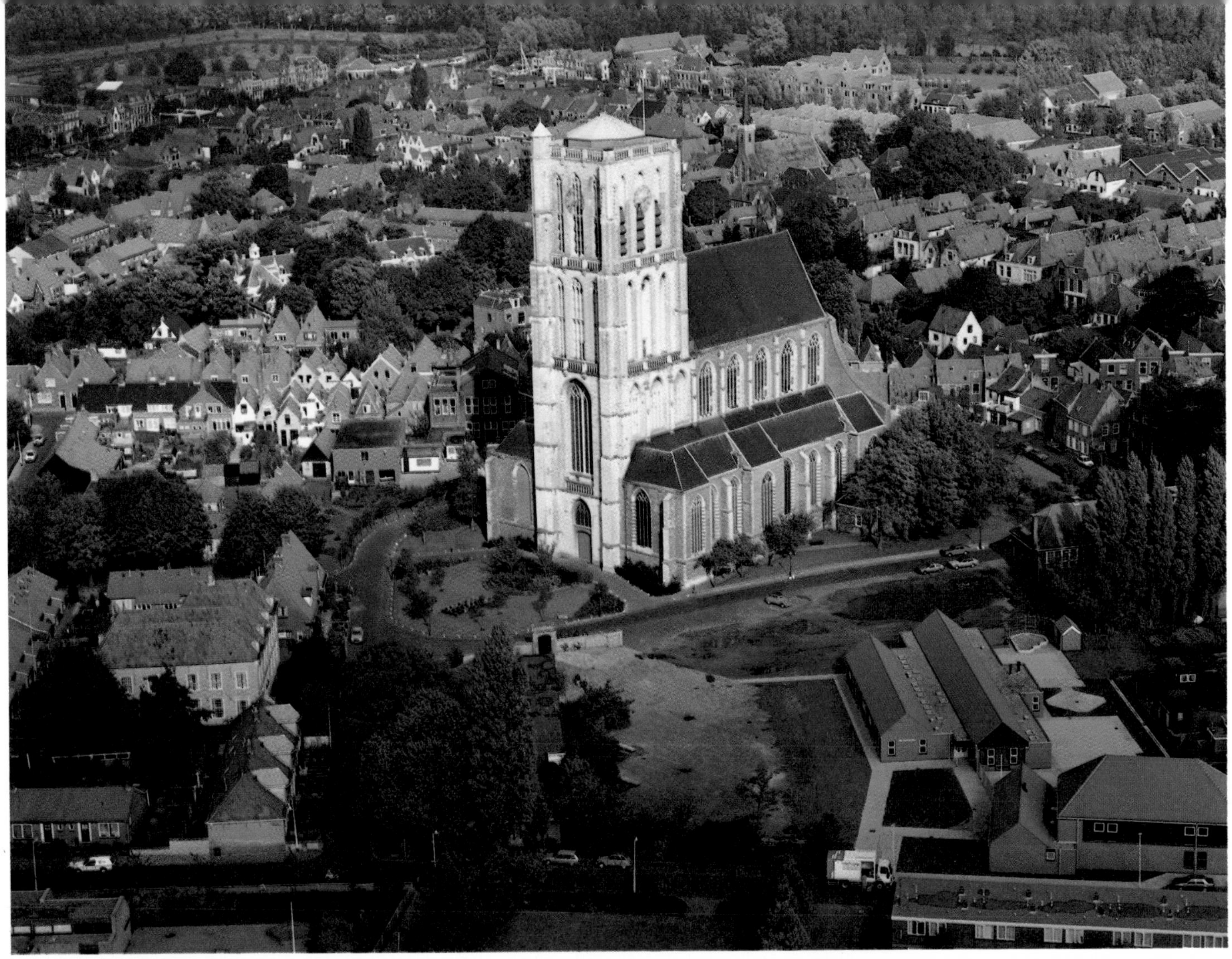

Again and again it is proven that Rijnmond is more than a world port. In 1417, Brielle began to build the St. Catharine's Church. However, the original plans – a tower crowned with an 8-sided cupola, complete with lantern – were never realized.
Instead a square-shaped, majestic tower was built, which due to its height of 57 meters, determined (and continues to do so) the silhouette of Brielle. In the tower hangs a carillon made by the famous French-Dutch bell-founder, Francois Hemony. It dates to the 1660s and has a splendidly rich sound, so typical of all Hemony chimes.
If you take the trouble to climb the tower, you will find it well worthwhile for its excellent view of the surroundings, clear out to the sea. Princess Mary Stuart took grateful advantage of this view when, in 1688, her spouse Prince Willem III crossed over to England in order to dethrone his father-in-law, James II.

The ancient centre of Brielle is marked by the outstanding spire of the Great or St. Catharine Church. When the Protestant captain, Lumey, entered Brielle by the north gate in 1572, this church became Protestant.

Hoek van Holland, Naaldwijk

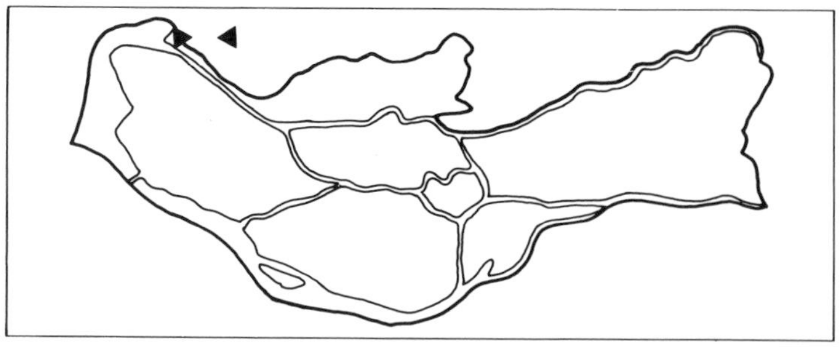

Beyond the Brielse Maas was Hoek van Holland, that is, until the construction of the Nieuwe Waterweg (1866-1872), when it was separated from the dune peninsula 'De Beer'. Hoek van Holland is now part of the municipality of Rotterdam. Its regular services to Harwich and its beach are the main features.

Where the path through the dunes, southward, is cut off by the Nieuwe Waterweg, lies Hoek van Holland, a partner-community and sea-side resort of Rotterdam. This has been a favourite recreation spot for years, and continues to be so.
During the 12th century, Zandambacht was founded on a dammed-off sand bank at the mouth of the Maas River. It was, apparently, such a beautiful little harbour town that the countess of Holland had a country home built there: Des Graven Zand. Others followed her example, such as the nobility, merchants and governors who had made their fortunes. Everywhere in Westland, these country estates could be found.
For their daily supplies of food, vegetables and fruit these country estates were entirely dependent upon themselves.
Horticulture grew into an art, for which Westland is still famous today. The same goes for Hoek van Holland, an important export harbour for horticultural products, which owes its importance as a port, mainly to shipping.
The steamship company, Stoomvaart Mij. ''Zeeland'', which has a regular service to Harwich, England, uses this harbour at the Maas River mouth as its departure point.

Slikkerveer, Rhoon

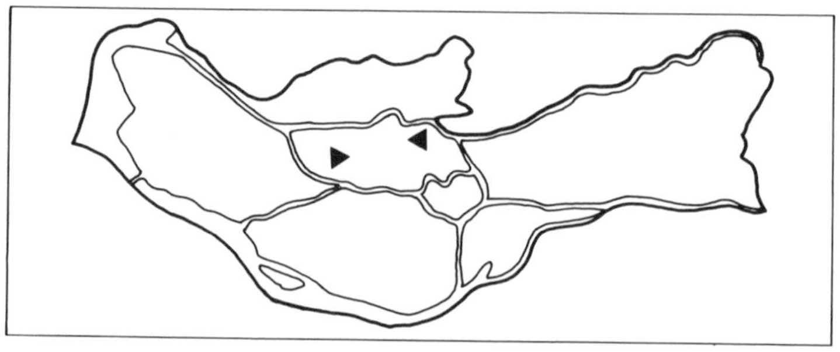

On the isle of IJsselmonde between Bolnes and Slikkerveer (both part of the municipality of Ridderkerk), a stone's throw from the Nieuwe Maas, is the manor-house 't en Donck'. Up to the present it has been inhabited by the Groeninkx van Zoelen family.

In between Bolnes and Slikkerveer, in the municipality of Ridderkerk, overlooking the Noord River, lies House of Donck (Huys ten Donck), a country house which is still used as a residence. Originally it belonged to the Regulars ten Donck or St. Maertensdonck, a monastery on the Donck River below Brandwijk in the Alblasserwaard.
Up until 1544, it is said to have been no more than a farmhouse. Records of the farm go back to 1443.
In 1544, the farmhouse was sold and torn down. In its place came a castle with 4 towers. In 1575, the Spanish ransomed and destroyed it, but in 1616 it was rebuilt and served as a country house. Then it was alternately sold, rented, sold again or bequeathed to other families. This it came into the possession of Catharina van Zoelen. In 1702, she married Mr. Cornelis Groeninx, gentleman of Ridderkerk and alderman of Rotterdam. Their son, Mr. Otto Groeninkx-van Zoelen, gentleman of Ridderkerk and Katendrecht and mayor of Rotterdam had the house torn down and in 1746 built the current great and stately Huys ten Donck in its place. The interior of Huys ten Donck is luxuriously decorated with stucco and sculptures. It is still occupied by the family, which in later years was raised to nobility.

For the most part, the Castle at Rhoon (Kasteel van Rhoon) was built in the 16th century. As if it were taken right out of a fairy tale, the castle is situated in the former centre of the village, to the north of the Rhoon metro station.
Apparently, some kind of a House of Rhoon was standing here back in the 12th century. Dirk VII, count of Holland, sold ''land under Peydrecht'' to Biggo van Duivelandt (a squire from Zeeland) and his cousins in 1199. (The Islands of South Holland which lay to the south of the Nieuwe Maas River, were also considered part of Zeeland, in those days.)

On the isle of IJsselmonde we find another great house, 'Kasteel van Rhoon', having a wide-spread and well-deserved culinary fame. The house is of great historical importance.

The purchased land still had to be diked in, which even then, was an expensive undertaking. In fact, it was a project which Biggo could not afford. Thus, Biggo and his cousins formed a ''partnership for the purpose of exploiting mud silt under Peydrecht''. The reclaimed land was then divided among the partners, into manors.
In 1329, the crumbling manor came into the hands of Boudijn II of Roden: the first lord of Roden or Rhoon. It remained in that family until 1683. Then, Hans Willem Bentinck, lord of Drimmelen and later count of Portland, bought the manor from the unfortunate Pieter IX of Rhoon, who had seen his downfall. In 1679, the unlucky squire had been forced to sell ''House of Pendrecht'' to the bailiff of Rhoon (a café located directly opposite the castle).
The Bentinck family considered this their country home and spent only a few weeks each year here.
Anthony van Hoboken, a Rotterdam ship owner, became the castle's owner in 1830. With his death in 1913, Edward van Hoboken was the last lord of Rhoon and Pendrecht.
The municipality of Rhoon started a foundation, which would dedicate itself to the dilapidated castle.
Now it serves a social and cultural function and in addition, is a fine restaurant.

Spijkenisse

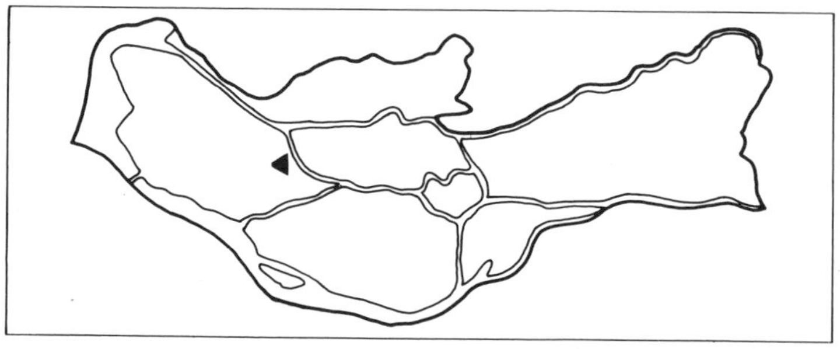

From Rhoon it is possible to travel to Spijkenisse by the underground system. At present Spijkenisse is the terminus of the Rotterdam underground on the south bank. This has not been random planning. Spijkenisse has been chosen as a growth town. The original population has grown due to people from Rotterdam coming to live here.

On the former island of Voorne, in the Vriesland Polder where now a new housing area stands in the municipality of Spijkenisse, traces of pre-historic settlements, dated roughly at 2200 BC have been found. This was possibly a seasonal camp for an ancient fishing community. Ruins from the time of the Romans have also been discovered in the area. Much later, during the Middle Ages, Voorne, Putten and Strijen made up a so-called free manor. The lords of Voorne were in charge of it. When this lineage died out in 1372, the manor fell into the hands of the count of Holland.
If, today, those people could see how their original manor has developed, they would turn over in their graves.
Since 1958, Spijkenisse has been the residential town for the Europoort-Botlek area and since 1977 a growth town. The population figures are expected to jump from 45,000 (in 1981) to around 67,000 (in 1990).
This expansion is in full swing in just about every sector.
Spijkenisse has a metro-connection to Centre City Rotterdam. The town is working hard to become a first-rate, dynamic residential and employment community. The policy of this municipality is geared toward reaching a balance between resident-workers and commuters.

FLYING, SAILING, ROLLING ALONG

Willemsbrug, Botlektunnel

Bridges, tunnels and ferries keep the river-crossing traffic in the Rijnmond conurbation moving. This is critical to a world harbour. Rotterdam has led harbour development; the Maastunnel was the first underwater tunnel in The Netherlands, and the latest achievement is the Willemsbrug.

Bridges, tunnels and a few ferries keep the traffic in the Rijnmond area moving smoothly, both over and under as well as on the river. This is of great economic importance. Rotterdam did not hesitate to take the first steps. Back in 1937 contruction began on the first underwater tunnel in The Netherlands, the Maastunnel. Bridges, tunnels and ferry boats are indispensable links in the north-south traffic.

The Willemsbrug, with its alluring cable work, lies in the heart of Rotterdam and serves to connect both Maas River banks. The combined efforts of designers, hydraulic engineers and steel construction engineers resulted in a high degree of perfection.

The Botlektunnel which goes under the Old Meuse River (Oude Maas) is seen on the above photo.
Modernly designed, this efficient passageway streamlines the heavy east-west flow of traffic between Rotterdam and Botlek, Europoort and Maasvlakte. The Botlek bridge, infamous for its slow-moving traffic is still important for the transport of dangerous loads. The nostalgic ferry on the Scheur, which makes the Maassluis-Rozenburg crossing provides many commuters with the shortest route to their places of work to the south of the Nieuwe Waterweg.

The Botlektunnel under the Oude Maas has met a great and urgent need. In the background you see the Botlekbrug, a bottleneck causing immense traffic jams. Now it is the route for the transport of dangerous material. The ferry from Maassluis to Rozenburg has an air of nostalgia.

100

de Brienenoord, Kleinpolderplein

Every Dutchman knows of the van Brienenoordbrug because hardly a day goes by when the radio does not mention its traffic jams. But rarely is mention made of the beautiful view which can be enjoyed whilst waiting in the queue on this bridge.

There isn't a Dutchman alive who hasn't heard of the Van Brienenoord Bridge. Hardly a day passes by, without the mention of this bridge's name on the traffic news bulletins.
At the time of its construction, it was expected to be the bridge to end all of the traffic jams in the Maastunnel and on the old Willemsbrug. Nowadays, it's known as THE bottleneck in the Rotterdam area.
Whatever problems it causes, the Van Brienenoordbrug is impressive proof of the skill of Dutch bridge builders. An eye-catcher from miles away, the slender steel construction spans the Nieuwe Maas as one mighty arch. If you have to wait in traffic on this bridge, you are assured a spectacular view.

The Kleinpolderplein near Overschie clearly shows how successful efficient channeling of traffic, at very busy road junctions, can be. This must have been designed by a meticulous monk with the patience of a saint. Like the decorative curlicues on a calligraphic document, the carriage-ways bend and stretch, widening and becoming more narrow, in all directions. Like industrious ants, the traffic hurries along over the hills and through the valleys of this masterpiece. The developers' dream and the builders' technical skill have attained praiseworthy success.

The Kleinpolderplein to the north-west of the Rotterdam ring road demonstrates the efficient system of motorways. Vehicles move hither and thither like busy ants.

Nederlandse Spoorwegen

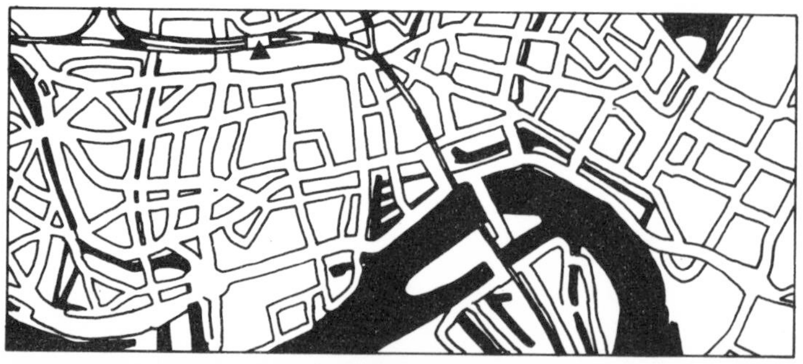

Central Station of Rotterdam. Not only a railway centre, but a centre for metro, tram and bus as well. An excellent meeting place, but sadly also one for the more questionable populace. The Boys' Choir of Rotterdam found a suitable home here in the bridge of the Esso tanker "Port Jerome", in the foreground.

For a leading world port to maintain its status, good inland connections are vital. Time is money goes for all phases of import, transit and export. The predominant factor is speed, as far as both the workers and the products are concerned.
The Netherlands Railroads Inc. (NS) also perceives this need for speed and efficiency. The NS nerve centre for the region, located at the Rotterdam Central Station, in the heart of the city, is the main terminal for trains, subways, trams and buses.
Unfortunately, the Central Station is also a meeting place for shady characters, who peddle contraband goods to their interested customers. The white ship's bridge at Stationsplein, taken from the Esso tanker "Port Jerome", serves as an original meeting place for the Rotterdam Boys' Choir.

Situated between Rotterdam and Dordrecht, in one of the remaining rural areas of IJssel monde, is Kijfhoek, the largest railroad shunting yard in The Netherlands. International freight trains and those headed for destinations within the country, are both marshalled here. This computer-controlled marshalling yard, which uses the most modern shunting techniques, may appear superfluous in the daytime. But in the evenings and during the night, the air buzzes with activity. When most people are resting after a hard day's work, Kijfhoek comes alive.

It may seem that Rijnmond can only be described in superlatives. This time: the biggest shunting-yard, ''Kijfhoek''. It is situated on the Rotterdam-Dordrecht railway line, in the middle of the rural area of IJsselmonde.

Metro

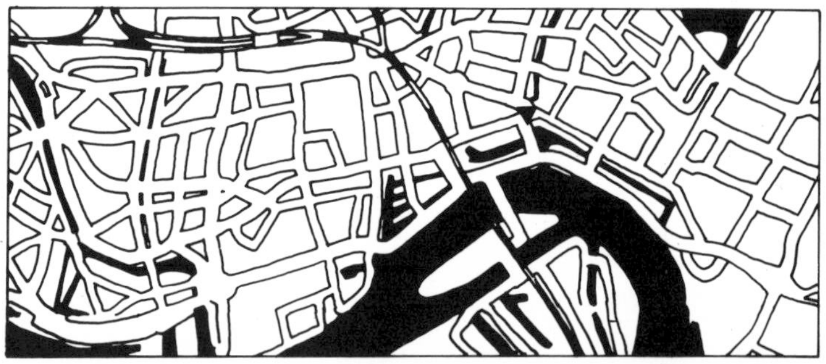

Where once the eastern part of the old city walls of Rotterdam stood, the Oostplein metro station is located. Here, under Oostplein lies an intricate system of cables, tubes and pipes. This super-modern station has two pedestrian tunnels with 5 entrances leading to them, including connections to the station hall. This allows metro passengers to avoid the busy traffic square as much as possible. The underground walkways were made more attractive when shops opened up there. The station itself has an arched ceiling. The former archway of the Mariniers Barracks, located at Oostplein serves as an attractive decoration above the southern entrance.

Where once the eastern part of the old city ramparts was, now lies, under Oostplein, the underground station of the same name. The former entrance gate of the naval barracks in Oostplein now adorns the wall of the south entrance.

The western line of the metro is still under construction. Located under the Schiedamseweg, this will be a tunnel, made of pre-fabricated parts. For the time being, the Marconiplein metro station marks the end of the years of construction which went into the Rotterdam metro system.
The excavated building site which is 310 meters long, has a maximum width of 36 meters and a depth of 9-10 meters, is a troublesome obstacle to the flow of traffic. However, as far as that goes, the people of Rotterdam are quite used to traffic problems. Countless temporary detours had to be set up, in order to keep traffic moving as steadily as possible. The construction plans for the metro station allow for a possible extension of the line into Schiedam, but that will have to be put off until better times to come.

The new east-west line of the underground ends at present, on Marconiplein. But this line may well be extended to Schiedam in the future, if Schiedam is willing to accept the line and the station.

Centraal Station

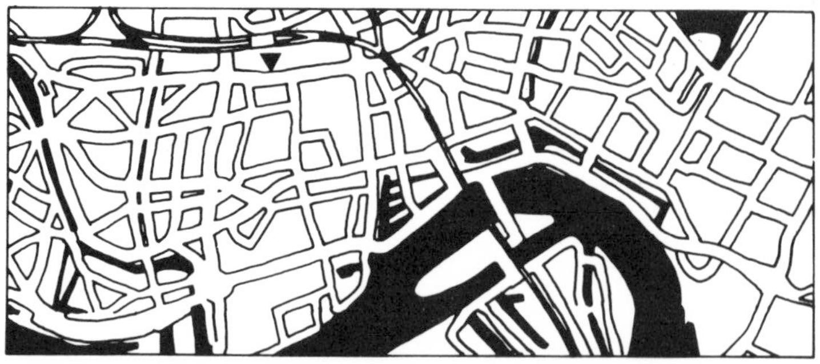

The R.E.T. (Rotterdam Electrical Tram) is the company responsible for Rotterdam's public transportation system. It is a municipal company, in charge of tram, bus and metro lines.
The hundreds of thousands of commuters, who make daily use of public transport little realize the organization which goes into making such a complex system function property. For most of them, buying their tickets is their only concern. The R.E.T. does its utmost to see that commuters get to their destinations as quickly as possible.

Central Station of Rotterdam.
In the foreground the bus station for regional transport. Beyond, the tram station and the station for city transport. The entrance to the underground is just below the latter. It seems to be a quiet moment of the day. Behind the bus station, (on the right), the Post Office is visible.

In fact, they go one step further and decorate the vehicles to make them as attractive on the outside as they are efficient.
The Rotterdam Foundation of Art took the initiative in arranging for municipal commissions to be given to artists on a regular basis for painting not only the sidewalks and plain walls but the trams, as well. The finished products are often startling.
Station Square in the heart of the city, is the starting point from which the trains, trams, metro and buses depart and fan out in all directions.
In fact, even the station for the regional bus service (run by Z.W.N.) is located at the Central Station, at the foot of the main Post Office building. This centrally located public transport system entices commuters to use it to its fullest.
Artist Louis van Rode's mural decoration on the post office's outside wall peers down on the activity taking place around it.

The painted trams of Rotterdam must seem a ludicrous sight for many of the people coming to Rotterdam for the first time.
The thought behind it is to give artists from Rotterdam the opportunity to bring their art among the people in a meaningful way. The government is subsidising this project.

108

Zestienhoven, Rotterdam Airport

Trade and industry of Rotterdam have had a fierce struggle to keep the airport of Zestienhoven running. Great pains have been taken to convince the municipality of its necessity. Its main activity to maintain a regular service to England.

Since the establishment of Zestienhoven Airport in 1956, this Rotterdam airport has created quite a stir. Rather curiously, not everyone was delighted with this decision. Several groups of protesters waylaid its continued existence. Even the municipal authorities themselves threatened, several times, to close down the airport. But how can the world's largest port function properly without an airport. Apparently there are continual conflicts of interest in this case, which do not allow for healthy competition between the Dutch airports. Is this what they call ''the game of political aviation''?

Without a doubt, Zestienhoven is an important stimulus to Rijnmond's economy. Now that the cries of protest have lessened, everything possible is being done to make up for lost time. Despite everything, the Rotterdam airport has almost managed to reach its 30th birthday.

The excellent water, road, rail and even pipeline connections provide Rijnmond with optimal access to the hinterland. Noting that Rotterdam has 10 railway stations makes one realize how important it is for Zestienhoven not to fall behind.
Zestienhoven is a very complete airport where numerous companies are located, including Aerocamera – Bart Hofmeester bv, responsible for the photographs which appear in this book. Every airport is a tourist attraction. Zestienhoven is no exception. Many enjoyable hours can be spent watching the planes coming and going. The café-restaurant, which offers a pleasant view of the runway, provides a special treat for young and old alike. Here you can expand your horizons as you let your thoughts carry you away to faraway places.

There are quite a number of companies which have settled on the site of Zestienhoven. Of course, the number of flights cannot be compared with that of an international airport like Schiphol. But it is growing and the interest in its potential is increasing. Its revaluation in the region is in progress at the moment.

Ferries

Though the Batavier line is no longer running from Parkhaven to England, there are other alternatives in Rijnmond, such as the car ferry to Hull. Thus the North of England is not far from a terminal in Europoort.

The slogan ''Rotterdam – Gateway to Europe'' is surely felt no more intensely than in the Benelux haven. Located in Europoort, this harbour houses two terminals for roll on - roll off ferry services to England.
Coordinating their activities at the Benelux haven and using the modern jumbo-carriers Norland and Norstar, North Sea Ferries, among others, maintains a daily ro-ro ferry service to Kingston upon Hull. They carry car passengers and foot passengers, as well as trucks of every size. These jumbos bring the Midlands and the North of England, Scotland, Wales and Ireland nearer to Rotterdam.
In fact, this method of transportation brings more than 25 million people in Great Britain and 70 million on the European continent closer together.
As the jumbo docks and its huge back doors swing open, one really gets the feeling that he is entering Continental Europe by the Rotterdam gateway.
Townsend Thoresen also docks in the Benelux haven, but there are numerous others as well. Rotterdam has many ro-ro facilities on Maasvlakte, in Hoek van Holland and in the Eem, Waal and Merwe Harbours.

At the Quick Dispatch Car Terminal most of the Japanese cars roll off the huge square ships right onto the immense parking lot, as if it were an extension of the famous Japanese conveyor belt. From the car parks the vehicles are loaded onto specially designed semi-trailers and railroad cars, destined for various European countries. In fact this terminal at Brittanniëhaven is the second of Quick Dispatch Company's Rotterdam locations. The first terminal, at Eemhaven, is still in use as well. Seaport Terminals b.v., in addition to its Eemhaven location will have a terminal for container ships here, as well.
The large car ferries could hardly be considered streamlined, and they pick up a considerable amount of cross wind. Complaints that the Eemhaven was easier in which to manoeuvre, led the municipality to conduct a special study. The solution was the construction of a gigantic wind screen measuring 1,700 meters long and 25 meters high. Supposedly, this will prevent the Calandbrug from receiving nasty thrusts.

Strictly speaking, this particular item does not belong under the heading "Everything rolls, flies or sails", but this does give an indication of what is moving on the Dutch roads.

Holland America Line

This book has not taken a particularly retrospective view. But coming to the end of this chapter it seems inevitable. It shows the end of the heydays of passenger shipping, two decades ago. Once again you can see the HAL (Holland America Line) in action.

On Wilhelminakade, at one time the location of the Holland-America Lines, many heart-rending scenes took place in the distant past. From here thousands of emigrants from Eastern and Western Europe departed for the New World, to start a better life. Shortages, religious persecution and progoms drove this ragged army to such extremes.

In the years that followed World War II, emigrants made up a large percentage of the passenger list on the H.A.L. ships which crossed the ocean to the U.S.A. and Canada. However, their economic situation was much more secure than the earlier emigrants.

The airplane eventually took over the passenger traffic and the sonorous tone of the passenger ships like the ''Rotterdam'' and the ''New Amsterdam'' have beenn silent ever since. Truly a shame for the Maas city!

In 1974, under pressure of unusually bad financial circumstances, H.A.L. sold its entire container shipping division to a foreign concern. H.A.L. Trust moved its headquarters to Bermuda. Currently, H.A.L. offers an extensive choice of cruises on luxury liners, departing from the United States.

HOUSING AND RECREATION

Delfshaven

Delfshaven, now part of Rotterdam, started out as its competitor. In the church of the Pilgrim Fathers, a magnificent centre of the beautifully preserved historic part of this town, a stained glass window commemorates the Pilgrim Fathers whu sailed from here in 1620.

During the Middle Ages, Delft decided that it did not want to be dependent on the ports of Rotterdam or Schiedam for its expanding export trade. Thus, the town dug themselves an open channel out to the sea, called Delfshavense Schie. The mouth of this channel became known as Delfshaven, which threatened to swallow up the mother city itself.
On 22 July 1620, the Pilgrim Fathers, mostly English weavers, sailed from Delfshaven at the site of this church, pictured here, in the "Speedwell", bound for North America and a new life.
Freedom of Religion was their driving force. Every year on Thanksgiving Day (the fourth Thursday in November) the American community in Rotterdam gathers at the Old Church or Pilgrim Fathers' Church (built in 1456) to recall this historical time. The Pilgrim Fathers are seen as the founders of New England.
In 1886, Delfshaven became a part of Rotterdam.

And this is the exterior of the Pilgrim Fathers' church. It dates from 1456. Every year on Thanksgiving Day (end of November) this church is the meeting place for the American community in Rotterdam which recalls that historic day of 22 July 1620.

Oude, nieuwe wijken

Rotterdam is a city of contrasts. In politics, in trade and industry, as well as in town planning. In the somewhat easy-going south district, in the neighbourhood of the Beijerlandselaan, is the Kiefhoek quarter. This, the brain-child of eng. J.J.P. Oud, immediately catches the eye.

Rotterdam is a city of contrasts: large and small-scale urban construction projects, maxi and mini-sized enterprises, as well as being politically variegated.
Amid the middle-class style buildings in Rotterdam-South, near Beijerlandselaan, you can't miss the Kiefhoek district.
This is the brain child of the engineer J.J.P. Oud, expert townplanner and publicist, who served as the architect of this municipality from 1918-1933.
Mr. Oud's younger brother was, at one time, mayor of the city of Rotterdam.

This progressive architect evolved ideas, which were known as "International Style" and built, among others, the districts of Spangen, Tussendijken, Oud-Mathenesse and Kiefhoek, in this style.
It is a very functional, timeless form of building.

The attractively renovated White Village on the boundary of Rotterdam and Schiedam is in stark contrast to the skyscrapers which house Euro-Point, at Marconiplein. It appears as if the quaint little houses are about to be overtaken by the huge office buildings in the background.
In former times they were intended to be temporary housing.
It looks like they have stood the test of time and they probably have several more good years left.

The attractively restored Witte Dorp (White Village), forming the border between Rotterdam and Schiedam, makes a contrast to the sky-scrapers of Euro-point on Marconiplein. Here it is not so much the creation of the architect which is striking, but the contrast.

Ahoy, Zuidplein

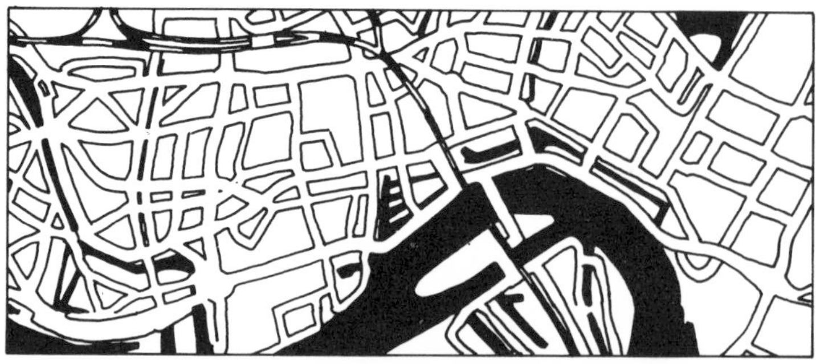

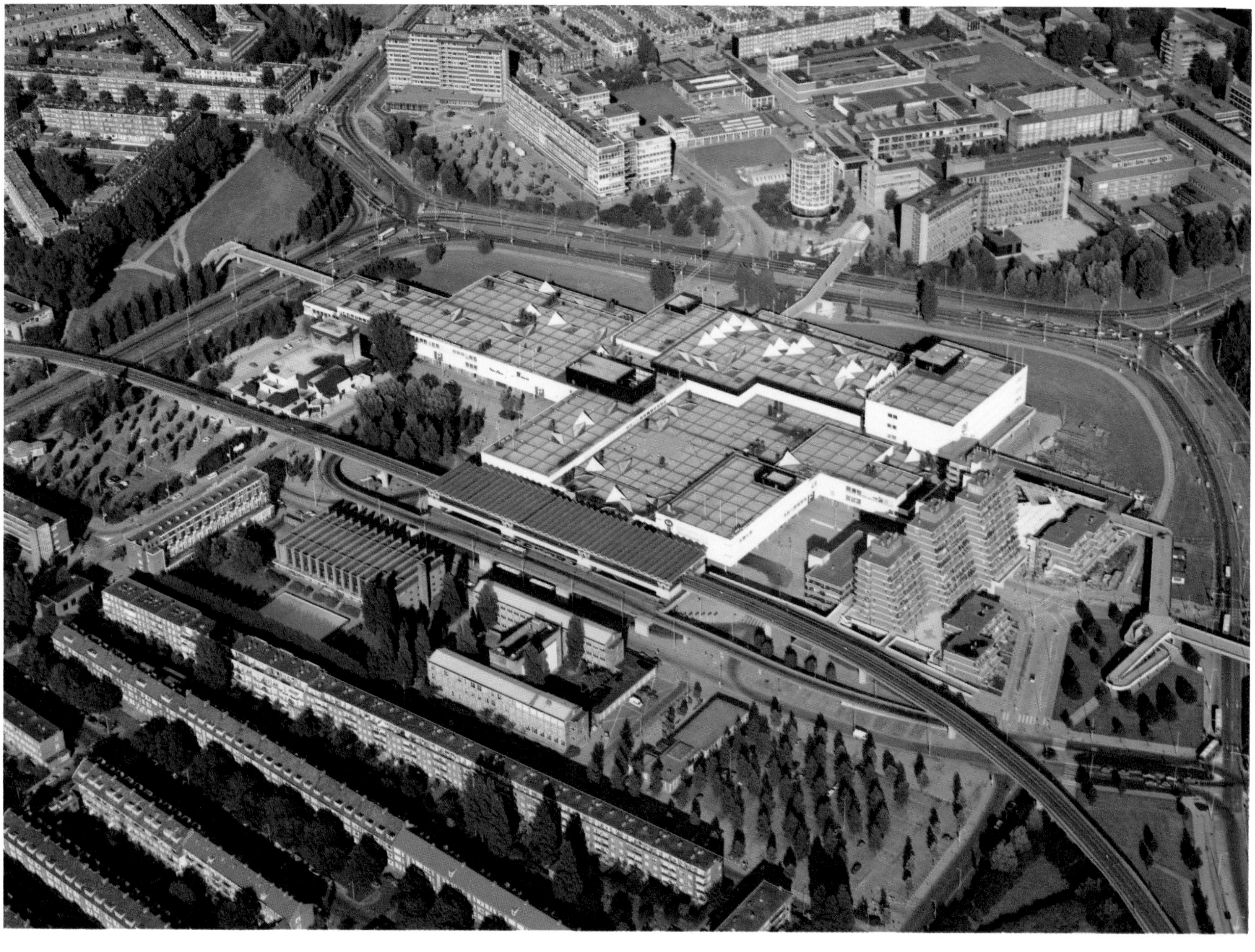

Next to the Ahoy-complex is the Zuidplein shopping centre. It is connected to the former by an elevated walkway. Here are also the metro station, the city-bus station and the station for the regional buses. All of them combine to bring the Ahoy and its surroundings within easy reach.

There is a time and a place for everything, which goes for Rotterdam as well. The people of Rotterdam are hard workers but they also love to be entertained. The working-city, Rotterdam's nick name, has been richly endowed with after-work activities. Movies, theatres, museums, cozy restaurants and pubs are too numerous to name individually. As if that wasn't enough, the city joined in the planning of outdoor recreational facilities for the Rijnmond area. And Rotterdam did still more. In the heart of Rotterdam-South (near Zuidplein, to be exact) a unique building complex was put up, called Ahoy.

The congress centre has all the necessary facilities at its disposal, which international standards demands. Ahoy is truly a phenomenon. On Zuidplein, opposite of Ahoy and connected to it by an over-pass bridge, is the enclosed shopping centre called Zuidplein. Refreshingly air-conditioned in the summer, and comfortably heated in the winter, shopping here is always a pleasure. The shops located here offer their customers a rich assortment of articles, that is second to none, not even to Coolsingel, Lijnbaan and Beursplein.

A large parking garage affords plenty of space for the cars of busy shoppers.
Ahoy and Zuidplein Shopping Centre are located in the immediate vicinity of the highway leading out of Rotterdam towards the Southwest of Holland. Both complexes are well-known far outside of the local area. The fact that the Zuidplein metro station has been built right into the shopping centre gives shoppers a direct route to the heart of Greater Rotterdam.
Ahoy attracts about a million visitors each year. The sports palace has seating for 6,000 spectators and is open to all kinds of events: sports, games, circuses and concerts. The permanent cycle-track is the starting point for the 6-Day International Race.
The exhibition halls vary in size from 900 sq. m. to almost 5,000 sq. m., with a total of 20,000 sq. m. of space.
Ahoy is a concrete wonder. It's not surprising, then that its architects were presented with the European Steel Award.
The names of the exhibition halls refer to well-known harbours of Rotterdam, such as the Eem, IJssel, Maas, Leuve and Schiehaven. These halls are also ideally suited to concerts, both of classical music and of modern music.

There aren't many people in Rotterdam who have not visited the Ahoy at least once in their life. Far outside Rotterdam this gigantic hall with its sports, conference and exhibition facilites has widespread renown.

Stadion, Marathon

A little further to the south of the city lies the stadium, the 'Kuip of Feijenoord'. When Feijenoord wins the national league, the shouting and singing can be heard as far away as the Coolsingel. It is traditional to follow such a victory with a reception at the Town Hall.

Rotterdam is strongly attached to her football teams. During international matches, the cry "Hup, Holland, hup!" can be heard rising above the Feijenoord stadion while during local games of the national league, the football anthem "Hand in hand, kameraden" is belted out.

If there's a win, droves of enthusiastic supporters swarm on to the field in an emotional display of gratitude to their sports heroes. Things get pretty hot at that point but the professionals know it's all part of the game.

When Monday morning rolls around, it's hard to get down to work before first comparing the latest sports results, in particular those of football. Depending on their performances, the favorite players are praised to the highest heavens or cursed to the depths of hell.

All of Rotterdam breathes the excitement of the trying 40 km Marathon. Center city turns completely topsy-turvy.
The Coolsingel, where start and finish lines are, is packed with spectators.
Nobody worries about the fact that the city's traffic is utterly disrupted. The traffic police just shake their heads at the whole situation. The buses, trams and cars quickly find out that it's every man for himself.
A 40 km jaunt of this kind is quite something and sports photographers really live it up trying to get unique shots from all angles. Cranes come in handy here for catchy photos that line the sports pages.

On Coolsingel another event takes place: the start and finish of the marathon. Of course, every town with some civic pride wants to host such an event. Our photographer was sitting even higher than those in the tall crane.

Het Park

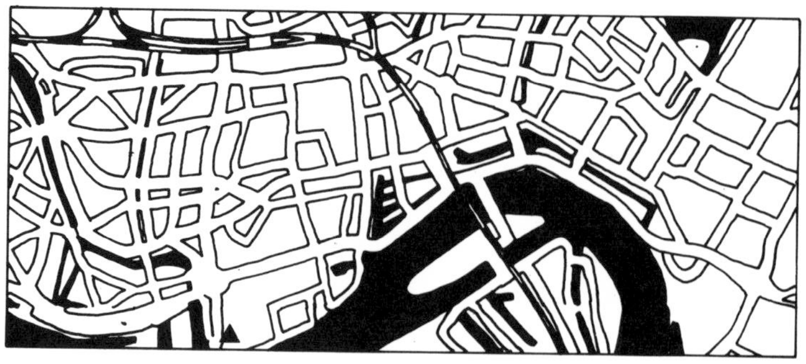

The oldest, genuinely-Rotterdam park is ''The Park'' between Dijkzigt and Nieuwe Maas – truly an oasis!
The Euromast, in the background, raised to double its original height in 1970, stands faithful watch over her park and takes delight in the colorful tulips at her feet.
In ''The Park'' whether in winter, spring, summer or fall, each season has its own charm. Even ice-covered crooked tree trunks shivering alongside of the ponds, do not in the least detract from the beauty of ''The Park''.

The Euromast shows that 'Het Park' (the park) is really the centre of the city. It is bordered by the Dijkzigt hospital on one side and the Nieuwe Maas on the other. In the course of the years the city has nibbled off quite a lot of its length and width. But this nibbling-off process now seems to have been halted.

Relatively speaking, Rotterdam is scantily endowed with parks and other public gardens. It amounts to 1,800 hectare altogether and that's nothing to brag about. Where there's nothing to be had, there's nothing to be gained.
Thus, it was no surprise that inter-municipal recreation committees began looking for possible locations elsewhere in Rijnmond. This is how recreational areas along the Brielse and Oude Maas Rivers, around the Rotte Lakes and near Westvoorne and Bernisse came to be.

We are fortunate to have such a patch of quiet in the centre of a city. There is no urgent need to rush off to the Brielse or the Oude Maas to get a bit of fresh air. Much has been done to extend the area of wood and parkland for the city.

Kralingen

Although Rotterdam may not have an overabundance of parks, public gardens and the like, what it lacks in quantity, it makes up for in quality. Take, for example, Kralingen Wood and Lake (Kralingse Bos). The Kralingse Bos was planted on the 26 million cubic meters of sand which was dug out to make the Waalhaven. Now surrounded by heavily populated residential areas, a combination of woods and lake of this scale is unique. The easily accessible lake lends itself well to wind surfing. Challenged by a breeze, spurred on by the wind, enthusiastic sportsmen can surf to their hearts content.
Of course, other water sports are represented here as well.
The beach areas are excellent for swimming, while those interested in soaking up some sun find the meadows just perfect. The quality of the water is acceptable to good.

The Kralingse Plas in wintertime. There is the fun of ice-skating for many. The tobacco mills, the Ster and the Lelie, are still here, and snuff is still milled here. The Ster dates from 1866, was destroyed by fire is 1962, and in 1968 was brought into operation again. The Lelie dates back to 1740.

In the Kralingse Bos, running along the east bank of the lake, is a bridle-path which leads to a riding-school on Kralingse Weg.
Golf used to be a sport reserved for the elite, upper class. Now it is enjoyed by a broader group of people. Golf means exercise as well as relaxation, excitement as well as rest, and is played in completely natural surroundings. Kralingse Bos has its own golf course, as well. Unexperienced players should keep clear of the course, though. The stone-hard little golf ball is capable of unusual stunts. As winter sets in, ice-skaters take over the frozen lake. The fact that you have to put up with traffic jams to reach it, doesn't deter too many people.
The two windmills, Ster and Lelie, just let the hustle and bustle pass them by.

The Kralingse Plas in summertime. It is not always as quiet as it seems now.
As a contrast we look back on the famous pop festival of Kralingen, witnessed by the Ster and the Lelie.

Rotte's Mannenkoor
Boymans, Doelen, Blijdorp

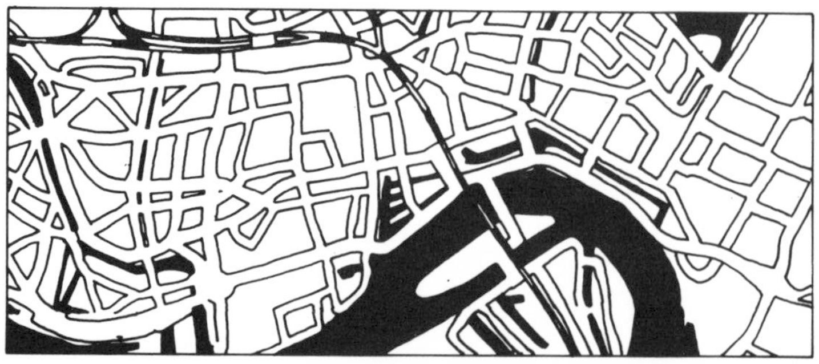

The Rotterdam male choir, which has gained wide popularity, is giving a concert in the St. Laurens Church. This church is being used more and more often for cultural activities.

Rotterdam is a city of hard workers. At one time, comedian Wim Kan swore that in Rotterdam, all shirts were sold with the sleeves already rolled-up. True Rotterdammers are few and far between. At the beginning of the 19th century there was a large migration from the country to the city, causing a sharp rise in the city's population. This was the case, again, between 1870 and 1930: all due to the insatiable need for workers in the harbours and on the docks. Characteristically the typical Rotterdammer is not considered to be too refined, yet there is a great demand for culture in all of its varied forms. Rotterdam has several good theatres. The AHOY complex is well-known for its concerts by popular performers.
One thing they're proud of in Rotterdam are their choirs. There's a spot in the heart of every upright citizen of Rotterdam for the Rotte's Male Choir. This choir performs regularly in the St. Laurens Church, which is made available for cultural events, as well. In addition, the organ recitals held in this church draw a wide audience.

The Doelen is one of the most modern concert and congress centres in the world and is best known for its fine acoustics. This gives Rotterdam a high-ranking position in the field of music. It is the home of the Rotterdam Philharmonic Orchestra.
Numerous museums add to the cultural richness of the Maas City: Boymans-Van Beuningen, the Historical Museum (located in the former Gemeenlandshuis van Schieland), the Non-European Folk Art Museum, the Historical Museum of the Royal Constabulary, the Prince Hendrik Maritime Museum and the Museum of Natural History.
Unfortunately, our space is too limited to give a complete listing of the Rotterdam Art Galleries.
More poetically-inclined souls will not hold it against us if we don't include a picture of Poetry International. After all, poetry is meant to be heard and not seen.
What we shall indeed include is a photograph of the baby elephant at Blijdorp Zoo. It may not be as culturally stimulating but it is truly heartwarming. This, in fact is a milestone in history: the first elephant ever born in captivity.
Somehow Rotterdam always has to be first.

The Boymans-van Beuningen Museum with the monument to G.J. de Jongh in the foreground Next to this museum is the famous De Doelen concert hall. In the upper part of the photo the baby elephant born at the Blijdorp Zoo can be seen. Together this gives an impression of the leisure possibilities available to the people of Rotterdam.

Fireworks

The immeasurable crowd throngs to the city and the Maaskade on Noordereiland becomes a stage, the reflecting water of the Nieuwe Maas River – the footlights and "De Boompjes" district on the right river bank – an open air theatre.
Such a firework display was set off in 1984 during a visit of an official delegation from the Japanese city of Kobe, with which Rotterdam maintains friendly ties. Kobe, antipodal to the Maas City, once a modest fishing village, has grown into one of the most important harbours in the Land of the Rising Sun. In 1868, this development went into full gear when Japan opened its doors to the West. No wonder that the municipality of Rotterdam outdid themselves in welcoming Kobe's official delegation and in their honour, set the city on fire, in a manner of speaking. During this fireworks display, the approving ohs! and ahs! could only be drowned out by the banging, whistling and hissing of rockets, sparklers and other tours de force. Showers of sparks and hoards of Bengal lights coloured the faces of the elated audience. And underneath all of the bursting fireworks, the silhoutte of a modern metropolis presented itself in a gossamer light.
The new Rotterdam rises up, like the mythical phoenix bird, out of the ashes of the Second World War. Rotterdam: strengthened by adversity.

The fireworks at the Leuvense Hoofd gives us this fine view of the city. Another and unexpected dimension, offered by the Japanese twin-city of Kobe.

A NEW HUB OF AN OLD CITY

Coolsingel, Stadhuis

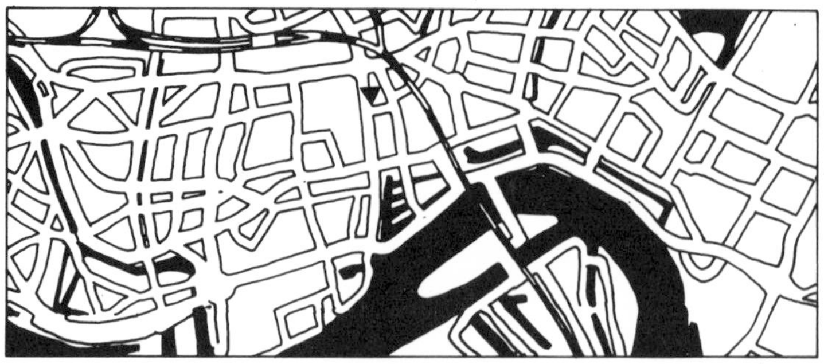

Coolsingel from north to south. The centre of post-war Rotterdam. When the re-building of Rotterdam began after the Second World War, the plan was to maintain the view of the HAL-ships. This has become irrelevant now.

The heart of this harbour city beats strongest between Hofplein and Churchillplein on the north-south axle of centre-city: Coolsingel. At one end the fountain on Hofplein, symbolizing an effervescent city and on the other, the towering building called ''De Coolse Poort'' with its deep purple tinted glass, form the boundaries of a world-famous promenade.
The eastern flank is made up of City Hall, the Post Office, the Exchange, C & A department store and Erasmus House. Bijenkorf department store, hotels, office buildings and banks line the western side.

Some older residents of Rotterdam complain that their city is not what its used to be before the war. Yet, would the older heart have been strong enough for these new times? Perhaps if things had happened differently, there would have been more time to gradually get used to all the changes and to understand their reasons.
Whatever the case may be, the present Coolsingel, spacious and efficiently set up, with it's small-scale restaurants, businesses and boutiques lining the wide sidewalks provide a friendly atmosphere to strollers and shoppers.

The City Hall, a creation of architect H. Evers, is one of the few buildings in centre-city which was left standing after the German bombing of 14 May 1940. It is located on the Coolsingel in what was the red light district at the turn of the century, called The Polder.
In addition to City Hall, the Post Office and Exchange Building survived the horrible Nazi aggression, which tore out the heart of Rotterdam.
In 1914, preparations were begun for the building of what was to be the largest city hall in The Netherlands. For example, 8,336 piles were driven into the ground, whereupon 15,376 cubic meters of concrete mortar, 1,500 tons of armament steel and 3,500 cubic meters of quarry stone had been used by the time the roof was put on in 1918. The new City Hall was officially opened when the first council meeting was held there on 1 September 1920.
The 71 ½ meter high tower is crowned with a dome covered with a sheath of green, oxidized copper. On the feast day of St. Margaret, 20 Juli 1948, the sounds of the carillon were first heard. The chimes, from 1921, were "removed" by the Germans in 1943 and have never been found again. When, close to Christmas, amidst the falling snow, the Norwegian Christmas tree with its hundreds of lights, silently announces the "Light of the World", the Coolsingel is permeated by a heartwarming atmosphere, that even the bleak time of the year cannot stint.

One of the very few buildings which survived the bombing of May 1940 was the City Hall, which was completed in 1920. It may not be very ancient, but in this post-war Rotterdam of concrete and glass it is an irreplaceable treasure.

Shopping Promenade

Coolsingel has two clearly visible boundaries: Hofplein to the north, dominated by the office block of Shell (on the far left-hand side) and to the south the purple office colossus, colloquially called 'the aubergine'.

No, it's not the road to Rome which runs from the Coolse Poort on Churchillplein to the Shell Building on Hofplein. But it IS the promenade which draws the people of Rotterdam together: Coolsingel. In all ways, shapes and forms, the nature of the Dutch people comes to light here: approving or disapproving depending on the circumstances.
Here the city parades, demonstrates and protests, as she goes on her way: inspecting, choosing and buying.
On and around the Coolsingel, the large department stores draw the attention of shoppers. But the smaller shops attract their share of customers as well.

Between magnificent bank buildings, department stores with wide assortments of merchandise and sky-high office buildings, the Rotterdammers have no trouble finding what they want. They are not that easily impressed. Shoppers show just as much (if not more) interest in the market salesman of leather goods on Beursplein as in the stylish novelties in a glittering show-window of an adjacent shop, which carries luxurious leather articles.
On a summer's day, the square across from City Hall, with its charming sidewalk cafés, invites weary shoppers to take a break. To look at the crowd of shoppers shuffling by, one wonders if an artist didn't happen to leave his colorful pallet behind. This sight is a welcome change in the daily routine.
And still, the green-roofed tower of City Hall faithfully keeps watch over this colorful crowd of people.
Every quarter of an hour, the tune of the carillon can be heard around the square.
The two bears (the sculpture at the corner of Lijnbaan) never tire of romping playfully.

On both sides of Coolsingel is the shopping district of Rotterdam. In the picture we see the Lijnbaan with City Hall in the background and Beursplein at the bottom. The beginning of Hoogstraat, the street along which, once the dam of the Rotte stretched. The birth of Rotterdam!

Laurenskerk

The St. Laurens Church has survived war-destruction. But since then the precinct has rarely been seen without scaffolding; this makes this picture rather peculiar as some ten years ago the scaffolding was taken down for a short time, to be replaced when it was enriched with the black cubic appendages.

In 1968, nearly 30 years after the devastating fire in May of 1940, the Reformed Church community of centre city Rotterdam returned to their Big Church, or St. Laurenskerk. It was indeed with the patience of saints and expert craftsmanship that the large-scale restoration took place. This is a late gothic cruciform basilica built with bricks with yellow sandstone bands, dating back to 1449-1525. The church consists of a west tower in four levels, a nave with side aisles, a transept and a choir with gallery. The exquisite brass choir-screen and the marble tombs of the Dutch naval heroes: Kortenaer, Van Brakel and Witte de With have been restored to their former splendour, just as has the Hemony-carillon from 1660. The bronze doors at the main entrance, under the tower are from the Italian designer Manzù. The main organ, as well as the two in the transept and the choir were built by the Danish organ-maker Marcussen.

The statue of Desiderius Erasmus (1469-1536) adorns the church square. This is the oldest statue in The Netherlands and was cast in 1622 by Hendrick de Keyser.

For centuries, this city on the Maas was planned in the shape of a triangle. An aerial view of the metropolis shows that it is still so. Schiedamse Vest, Coolsingel and Goudsesingel form the original city boundaries. The 16th and 17th century harbours, such as Wijnhaven, Leuvenhaven, Scheepsmakershaven, Haringvliet, Blaak, Boerengat and Buizengat had open connections to the river. The ships anchored there unloaded their goods right at the merchants' door step. In later years, many of these harbours were filled in or made available to Rhine barges and other inland ships. During the reconstruction of the city, after 1945, plans were made to concentrate businesses with similar functions in one area. Examples of this are the Groothandelsgebouw, the Industriegebouw and the banking buildings in the same area as the Exchange Building.

In front of the St. Laurens, Erasmus is standing on his pedestral, 'turning a page every hour', as the local boys say.
At top, another picture of the old city triangle, seen from the west. Coolsingel was the western most boundary of this ancient city.

Groothandelsgebouw, World Trade Center, Erasmusuniversiteit

The Rotterdam Commerce Exchange (N.V. ''De Beurs van Koophandel'') is owner and manager of the Stock Exchange Building (Beursgebouw) located on Coolsingel. Here, among others, the Insurance Echange, Commodities Exchange, Shipping Exchange, Chamber of Commerce and numerous offices and shops are found.
When the planned ''tower'' is built onto the Exchange Building, making it 88 meters (20 stories) high, this complex will serve, even more than before, as Rotterdam's national and international trade centre. The fact that its name will be changed to ''Beurs – World Trade Center'' convinces one of the new activities which will be taking place and the new character that this building will take on.
Above the glass roof of the large exchange hall, the suspended tower of the World Trade Center will be built. The oval-shaped extension is technically of the highest-standing.
Above the roof, supported by these pillars, the foundation for the new ''tower'' will be laid in mid-air.
The floor on which the records office is located resembles a bunker, with its 2 meter thick walls. The 65 meter high ''tower'' will snugly rest on a huge slab, made of armament steel, as if it were a ship's mast. This building is truly a daring escapade in Rotterdam's building ventures of the '80s.

Only by means of a photo of the architectural model can the latest plans for the extension of Rotterdam be shown. On top of the Stock Exchange building a gigantic spire is to be erected to include the World Trade Centre.

Other cities were quite envious in those years. The Groothandels-gebouw (designed by architect H. Maaskant) was finished in 1951. This is a complex of large caliber in which wholesale dealers in various lines of business have set up their showrooms and offices. Located in the immediate vicinity of Central Station, it serves as an ideal centre for buyers. It is easily accessible by public or private transportation and provides its own parking garage.

In 1973, the Erasmusuniversiteit Rotterdam (EUR) was founded. It represented a merger of the College of Economics (Nederlandsche Economische Hoogeschool) and the Medical Faculty, started in 1966. The EUR is a state university, the name of which honours Desiderius Erasmus (1469-1536), Rotterdam's greatest son: the scholarly humanist of his time, whose influence is still felt today. The stark, white Medical faculty on Westzeedijk can be seen from far and wide. Towering high above the city, it is a most exclusive construction. It even tends to overpower the nearby hospital, Dijkzigt ziekenhuis.

The Groothandelsgebouw on the Stationsplein was the first large post-war building.
For many years Rotterdam possessed only the Economic College, but after the arrival of the medical faculty to the Dijkzigt hospital this college was renamed Erasmusuniversiteit.

Modern housing

The building activities in the city centred chiefly on housing in order to bring its depopoulation to a halt. This housing complex was built on the Haagse Veer along the Rotte.

Disbanding the old-fashioned idea that a city's centre should only include local businesses, city planners considered new possibilities. In this respect, a great deal of imaginative designing has gone into the planning of housing areas in Delftse Vaart, Stok en Rotte. Every available inch of space has been used to its fullest potential. The apartments on the ground floor open onto terraces which extend out over the Rotte River. Even those living on higher floors of the building, have spacious balconies. Everyone's needs are met so completely that even the pub 't Swarte Schaep has nothing to complain about. At the turn of the century, this area, known as The Polder, was Rotterdam's red light district. At that time very colourful stories circulated about this area, even as far as Paris, where cabaret entertainers sang about ''le poldère''.
It's no wonder then, that Koos Speenhoff, in his ''Letter from a naughty girl'' wrote:
Hey Reds, what a shock you'll get
When you come back home
To see just what's become
Of the Polder you have known.

No, sir, the complaint on the lips of older Rotterdammers, that ''the ole city, she ain't what she used to be'' is nothing to worry about, in this case. The new city centre continues to undergo radical changes. Imagine the scope of modernization the older buildings would have had to be subjected to, to keep up with the times! Isn't the new facade still overshadowed by the unforgettable destruction with which the older buildings had to contend?
It's not only the spaces which for many years stood open in the heart of the city which are being filled in by attractive new neighbourhoods; the olders western section between Nieuwe Binnenweg and West Kruiskade also get their share of attention. Renovations and brand new buildings give this district a completely new look. On this subject, the area surrounding Sterkmanplein speaks for itself. The new homes on Josef and Gaffelstraat make its residents feel like they've been given a new lease on life.

The old western part of the city survived the last war fairly well, but the state of the houses seriously declined. Renovation on a large scale was the answer. As a mark of orientation: the topmost picture represents the Bouwcentrum and, below the Dijkzigt Ziekenhuis is visible.

de Marinier, Zadkine

There are strong ties between Rotterdam and the Marine Corps. When in May 1940, the threatening clouds of war burst over Rotterdam, the corps of the Marines, known as the black devils, courageously defended the bridges over the Maas River until the bitter end. Queen Wilhelmina singled out the corps standard with the Distinguished Service Order of Willem and conferred on the corps the motto ''Qua Patet Orbis'' (To all corners of the earth). The statue of ''The Marine'' which guards the spot where the Marine barracks stood prior to 1940, pays tribute to the brave performance of the corps during war-time (a salute to honour).

The ''Monument for a devastated city'', by the Polish-French sculptor Ossip Zadkine recalls the cruel and senseless destruction of the heart of Rotterdam. Its hands, despairingly raised toward heaven and its breast, rent open in anguish, represent the fallen. The wounds have healed but no matter how well the ''plastic surgery'' of ingenious town planners has tried to hide the scars, sometimes they still smart. A city can be compared to a human body, which feels old wounds, when the weather changes. And so it is with the master creation of Ossip Zadkine.

The mariner on Oostplein keeps watch over the Noordereiland, above which a thunderstorm is approaching. The old Willemsbrug can still be seen, before its disposal to the scrap-heap.
Zadkine's ''devastated city'' on Leuvehaven, the post-war symbol of Rotterdam.

Blaak

De Blaak, buzzing with building activity. In the middle of this historic centre of Rotterdam were constructed, within a very short time, the library, the residential tower with the pile-dwellings annexed, and the buildings along the Oude Haven and the Haringvliet.

Centre-city Rotterdam continues to make space available for building projects. The brand-new library, familiarly known as the building with tubes on it, was patterned after the George Pompidou Centre in Paris. Next to it is the tower-shaped apartment building, with its pointy roof, designed by the architect Piet Blom. The shape reminds one of the old-fashioned carpenter's pencil or maybe even a modern rocket, which is about to be launched. This tower-shaped building takes up very little space and yet offers a surprising number of apartments to one and two person households. This made it possible to build roomy cube-shaped pile-dwellings nearby.

Although taller buildings have altered Rotterdam's skyline in recent years, the ''White House'' is still a well-known landmark. When it was built in 1883it was Europe's first ''skycraper''. The 10-story office building on Geldersekade was Rotterdam's pride and joy. When the building of the railway tunnel commences the Blaak train station area will undergo radical changes. The mess created by this work will be indescribable. But the residents of this Maas City, are quite used to upheaval. It's been the same story through the years of post-war reconstruction right up to the recent building of the metro network.

This small square on the Oude Haven offers a futurist view with its pile-dwellings, constructed by the architect Piet Blom. ''Het Potlood'' (the pencil), as the people of Rotterdam call it, forms a beautiful contrast with these houses. The precinct itself has appropriately been named Overblaak.

Oude Haven

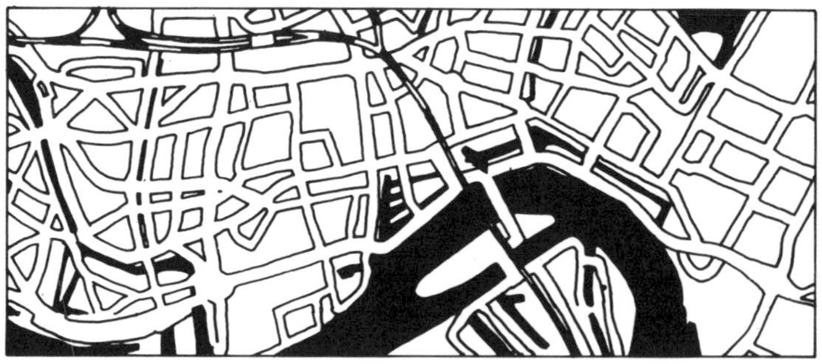

This shows the old harbour complex as the beautiful centre of past and present: no better ending for this book.
In the background some more well-known buildings which were shown earlier: the St. Laurens, the Town Hall, the White House.
Rotterdam and Rijnmond: let's meet again!

We conclude our photo-safari through the land of the silver belt with its golden clasp, in the Old Harbour (Oude Haven), known as the "cradle of Rotterdam". This area could be honoured in no better way than by the Open Air Inland Shipping Museum which is located here. The Koningspoort building slip, the sliding ways house, carpenter's sheds and old ships set the mood in which Rotterdam's history had its start, centuries ago. Yet Rotterdam continues to look forward to a future in which this part of the city will be very much alive.

*It's as if, from this harbour some force drifts to all parts of the world.
No matter where fate may lead you, you remain within its grasp.
It's as if, with her air and water and wind, she has reared us in breadth of outlook, to confront the shores of our future.
Whether you roam to Sydney or Cape Town, to Kobe or Baltimore, or travel to all corners of the earth, or travel all seas of the world, you never feel completely alone if here, you began your earthly days, with what, from childhood on, was near and dear to you.
That is Rotterdam.*

(Translated from "Rotterdam" by Jan Prins)

Zweth
Negenhuizen
Kandelaar
Zouteveen
Spoorbuurt
SCHIEDAM
Overschie
Kleinpolder
Holy Noord
Kethel
Spaanse Polder
Groenoord
Holy
Bijdorp
Nieuwland
VLAARDINGEN
Spangen
Oud-Mathenesse
Tussendij
Westwijk
De Gorzen
Nieuwe Maas
Merwehaven
Wilhelminahaven
Vulcaanhaven
Wiltonhaven
Heyplaat
Pernis
Eemhaven
Prins Johan Frisohaven
Prinses Beatrixhaven
Prinses Margriethaven
Prins W Alexanderh
Vondelingenplaat
1e Petroleumhaven
2e Petroleumhaven
3e Petroleumhaven
Oude Maas
Geulhaven
Botlek
Gadering
Nieuw Engeland
Westpunt
Centrum
Hoogvliet
POORTUGAAL